HOME MATTERS

Penny Wincer

How Our Homes Shape Us, and We Shape Them

photography by Penny Wincer
cover illustration by Lianne Nixon

quadrille

This book was written partly on and about the unceded, sovereign lands of the Wurundjeri people of the Kulin Nation and I pay my respects to Elders past and present. I acknowledge the Aboriginal and Torres Strait Islander Peoples who are the Traditional Custodians and storytellers of these lands. I honour Aboriginal and Torres Strait Islander Peoples' continuing connection to Country, waters, skies and communities.

For my Dad, Simon

Contents

Introduction: Why thinking deeply about our homes matters

I have lived in all sorts of homes. From the detached Australian houses of my early years, to New York City apartments, ex-council flat-shares, unconverted warehouses and now a 1930s terrace in South London. There is nothing particularly exceptional about the number or variety of homes I have lived in. But I have also seen the insides of more homes than I could possibly count.

During the first six years of my career, I was an assistant to fashion photographers in London and New York, where I shot in an endless parade of exceptional homes, which provided a setting for magazine covers, advertising and catalogues – from large, empty white Victorian mansions, to quirky, trinket-filled villas in Sicily. And then I spent 15 years as an interiors photographer, shooting for magazines and commercial clients.

Contrary to what many might assume, my favourites of the homes I spent time in were never the largest, the most expensive or the most luxurious. Those kinds of homes were often very dull and, luckily for me, I was barely ever hired for that kind of shoot. Bland, expensive, designed by a professional and not the owner, those houses always felt like a backdrop to me. A stage set, in which lives played out as a performance.

Homes tell stories. A home is the culmination of those who create them, where a person's history and present blur together. As a photographer, I'm invited into spaces that very few people outside of immediate family are allowed to enter. When I'm telling the story of a home, I am making choices about how this home will be seen by others. I may leave out some of the more intimate aspects of a person's home – the cupboard where things are hurriedly shoved out of the way; the office door pulled shut; the beloved armchair inherited from a grandparent, which sits in an unexceptional corner that doesn't make the cut. But I see it all, even if the viewer does not. And there is no bigger privilege than being allowed to spend time digging around other people's homes.

I was not initially interested in shooting homes. When one of the fashion photographers I worked for first suggested I shoot interiors, I scoffed at the idea. I was spending my time flying back and forth to New York, working for photographers shooting for British *Vogue*, Burberry, L'Oréal and Ralph Lauren. In the masculine world of fashion, where male photographers still dominated, I saw interiors as domestic, feminine and less prestigious – an internalised misogyny, which meant I saw it as somehow 'less than'. As a female assistant, I spent my time trying to downplay those aspects of myself. It was not that many years since hiring a female assistant would have been unheard of, and I was acutely aware of that, even if no one said it out loud.

But when I was asked to do a couple of small interiors jobs as a favour, I very quickly fell in love with shooting homes. I realised that telling the story of homes was like telling the stories of our lives. That my long obsession with films that exploited interior settings, such as Alfred Hitchcock's *Rear Window* (1954) and Wong Kar-wai's *In the Mood for Love* (2000), was partly because of the intimacy of those spaces that are usually hidden behind closed doors.

My favourite novels, too, were often based around homes. Every one of Jane Austen's heroines is either struggling to gain or hold on to a home. Elizabeth Bennet and her sisters will be turfed out of their home the moment their father dies. Anne Elliot finds herself homeless and drifting between her father's rented house in Bath and her sister's marital home, not really belonging anywhere. And Elinor and Marianne Dashwood are relegated to a small country cottage far from the grand house they were raised in because their elder half-brother doesn't imagine it matters to them at all. Arguably (and I think many academics would agree), some of the greatest novels written in the English language focus on domestic lives.

Despite this, I have found over the years that thinking about our homes and considering them in detail is often viewed as shallow and frivolous (unless it's specifically to improve their monetary value). While housing, and access to it, are considered important (though much-neglected) political topics, the aesthetics of our homes is not. It's considered a subject for the privileged middle classes, those who don't have to concern themselves with basic human dignities, such as having a roof above their heads and a warm, dry, safe space to live.

But the aesthetics of our homes, how we shape and decorate them, do matter, regardless of our financial and social circumstances. Even though some might not be particularly conscious of it, and perhaps not even that interested in it, that does not mean we are unaffected by it. Whether we are renters, homeowners, social tenants or in temporary housing, each one of us is altered by the environment that surrounds us.

Our homes shape us. They support us when the outside world might be challenging and hostile to be in. I would argue, in fact, that the home of someone who finds the world more challenging is even more important than that of those who can breeze through life, welcome in all kinds of public spaces. Private homes are places that can reflect and support who we are, so that we can safely be ourselves.

*

I share a small terraced house in South London with my two children, who are currently twelve and fourteen. We have lived here for over eleven years, nine of which I have been a single parent. It is, in many ways, a far cry from the homes of my own childhood in Melbourne. I have different concerns to those my own parents had. I have the typical time and financial constraints of a single, working parent and additional ones, too, as my eldest child is disabled. As a homeowner, though, I am also very privileged, with a manageable(ish) mortgage, in a neighbourhood I could no longer afford to rent in if I had to. I am definitely one of the lucky ones.

Over the years people have asked me if I get envious of the homes I shoot. I don't particularly, and that answer often surprises them. Many imagine that constantly photographing homes that end up in glossy magazine spreads must leave me feeling as though my own home is inadequate by comparison. But the privilege of telling the stories of these homes means that I see them inside and out. I see the beauty, of course, but I also see the cracks. I see how much work and money goes into them. I get a glimpse of the sweat and the time and the heartache that the homeowners have poured into them. I see the hassle and the compromises. I get to see a whole picture, with all its ups and its downs.

This bigger picture that I have been allowed to see has changed my mind about a few things over the years. It's made me reconsider the importance of size, cost, what we hang on to (and what we let go of), trends, ownership (emotional, as well as legal) and how we respond to the challenges in our lives, inside our homes.

Walking through these homes, camera in hand, is not the same as flicking through the pages of a magazine. The conversations I have had over the years (I do love to chat while I shoot) are often not the kinds of things that run alongside the carefully edited pictures in the magazines. But these conversations have changed my perspective many times.

In the following pages I invite you, the reader, to come with me into some of these homes. To follow me and my camera as we are invited in to have the kinds of conversations that have confirmed for me over the years that thinking deeply about our homes is far from frivolous. I would like to ask all of us to reconsider some perhaps long-held beliefs about our homes, to see them in a new light. About what might be most important and what might not be very important at all.

The homes in the following pages are all very different and, unlike those in most books about interiors, they do not follow a single aesthetic style. There are flats, suburban houses and farmhouses, urban and country. They are colourful and monochrome, large and small, simple and complex. The homeowners come from a variety of backgrounds but are mostly artists, designers and writers, all with a different sense of style. They do all have one thing in common. They all have homes that reflect their own needs, desires and lives. That reflect their values as well as some realities and compromises.

These are not perfect homes, and they don't need to be. The stories of our homes are the stories of ourselves. And that of course means they are flawed and full of challenges. But they are also filled with surprising outcomes, pleasures and love.

Sometimes, getting a glimpse into others' lives can help shift our perspective on our own. My home, which is both beautiful and filled to the brim with the kind of compromises that come from a lack of time and money, and the constant adjustments to meet my son's needs, is one that I have grown to love and embrace in part because of these challenges, not just despite them. It is the stories behind all the homes I have been in that have helped me to see this.

Homes are more than just places to take shelter. They are the places that hold us through all the ups and downs of our lives. And they can do so in many more ways than we might think. How does our past affect how we create our current homes and what can we gain by reflecting on that? How does colour make us feel and behave? Is it personal or universal? How much space do we really need? Is size at all important? How do we decide on the kinds of objects we hold on to, and what can or should we let go of? Does it even matter? Through conversations with a number of homeowners, I explore the nuanced answers to these questions. What you will find is not a straightforward set of rules to follow, but rather a series of questions to reflect on in the context of your own life and home.

Introduction

Thinking about our homes can help us understand ourselves and how much those homes can support us through life's challenges, as well as its many pleasures. They are one small part of the world we can have a little control over, when so much in our lives is outside of our control.

It has been one of the greatest privileges of my career to be invited to spend time in other people's homes – to hear the stories of precious objects and furniture, how layouts came into being and what inspired the colour on the walls and the plants in the garden. The homeowners in these pages have generously agreed to let me share some of the intimacies of their homes and their stories with you as I piece together the lessons I have learned and continue to learn from all the homes I have spent time in over the years. If all our homes tell a story, there are countless unique tales out there. These represent just a few.

Chapter One: The Memory of Home

Mooroolbark, Melbourne, and South London

Perhaps it is because I live in a country where I did not grow up, but I am fascinated by how the homes of our childhood shape our perception of home. I've had British friends tell me a house must have stairs or it's not a house. Or that anything built after 1945 is 'new'. As an Australian I find these ideas quite amusing, but I don't think they are particularly unusual beliefs in the UK, where much of the housing stock was created when cities boomed during industrialisation.

I have my own unusual ideas about home, too. I am still not really accustomed to hearing neighbours through the walls or having a washing machine in the kitchen. And what is the obsession with baths? I remember the builder who shook his head sadly at me when I asked him to rip one out of the miniscule bathroom in my first flat and replace it with a roomy shower. 'You'll never sell it on without a bath,' he warned.

Our ideas about what makes a home are more deeply embedded than perhaps we realise. Something I have come to understand when my own ideas of home haven't always matched up with those around me.

'There is only one place I really think of when I think about my childhood houses. Badgers Wood.'

Mooroolbark, Melbourne

I climb up the small wooden stepladder and pull the photo albums down from the highest shelf. They are fat and heavy, with pages that are sticky and covered in plastic sheets that make a ripping sound when you pull them back. I flip the pages. Under the shiny coating of plastic, I find what I am looking for. Home. There is only one place I really think of when I think about my childhood houses. Badgers

Wood. A white weatherboarded house in the outer eastern suburbs of Melbourne, which sits on an acre of garden on a quiet unpaved road. It is Australia, but the gardens are a mix of English and native – built, like all the houses on this hidden road, by English-born landscape designer Edna Walling, who created this 'village' on the outer edges of Melbourne in the 1920s.

In my mind, I walk down the narrow, unpaved road pitted with refilled potholes that the residents of the street fix themselves twice a year in working bees. The trees tower overhead, arching and reaching over to create a tunnel. They are deciduous and native, a mix I am well used to in my childhood in a colonial country. European plants imposed on Naarm* soil by settlers. Hydrangeas and agapanthus grow in the red earth that I was told as a child gives this particular suburb, Mooroolbark, its name. Our street, Bickleigh Vale, is named after a village in Dorset, and our house, Badgers Wood, after an animal that doesn't exist on this continent.

Its white-painted, wood casement windows are a throwback to the designer's origins, but the corrugated tin roof is as Australian as roofs come. Down the steps there is a barn-style kitchen door that can open in two parts. My parents built this kitchen extension when I was three years old. It juts out from the original cottage and has multi-paned casement windows running around two sides. Underneath the windows is a slouchy old sofa which the dogs lie on; my brothers and I are often found there, too. In the centre of the room is the scrubbed wooden kitchen table, the head of which always belongs to Mum, who springs up and down from the table at mealtimes like a jack-in-the-box and likes to be close to the kitchen. The fitted kitchen is made entirely of warm pine wood, including the tongue-and-groove walls. The floor beneath my feet is cool slate. Not the rectangular dark-grey kind typically found in the UK but the warm, earthy tones and irregular shapes of Castlemaine slate, mined in central Victoria.

*Naarm is the Traditional Place name for Melbourne in the Woiwurrung language of the Kulin Nation.

By the freestanding electric stove, where my mother's roast lamb and lasagne are made, is the built-in pantry, which is big enough to hide from my brothers in and, later, the place where I can pull the long, curly cord of the telephone for privacy.

Through the glass-panelled wood door by the fridge, I come to the old part of the house. Its ceiling follows the slope of the roof. The panelling surrounding the long row of cottage windows is stained dark and each window is topped with scalloped Roman blinds in a creamy lace. It is a narrow room with a dark dining table, bearing the etching of homework where we have pressed too hard on our paper. The accidental ('8 × 8 = 64') and the more deliberate ('Ash Was Here'). As I reach the far end of the room it widens into the sitting room. Its pitched ceiling makes it the most gloriously noisy room in the house when it rains. With its stone fireplace, painted beams and whitewashed walls, it is easy to believe the story that Edna Walling based it on (and named it after) Badger's cottage in Kenneth Grahame's *The Wind in the Willows*.

Back through the dining room and up the stairs at the far end, I run my fingers along the rough texture of the yellow floral wallpaper. To the right of the landing, with a door so small you could mistake it for a cupboard, is my bedroom. Inside the slope-ceilinged room I am the only family member who can stand up fully straight. My low wooden bed sits in the triangular window. Under my white broderie anglaise quilt, I read by torch light. It is the perfect spot to watch for my friends from the street who come knocking to see if I can come out and play. There is not the ceiling height for a wardrobe, so everything is in a chest of drawers. It is a perfect child's bedroom, too uncomfortable for grown-ups to be in for any length of time.

This home is still vivid in my memory. I look around me now and see vestiges of it playing out in my own grown-up home. I live in a small pebble-dash 1930s terraced house in South London and some might say it's a far cry from the idyll I grew up in. But I see so many similarities. The blousy hydrangeas and roses that droop over my front path. The cosy front room, which I refuse to make open-plan. The different textures and natural materials that I am drawn to and have throughout the house. The windowsill behind the kitchen sink, which has accidentally replicated my mother's casual shrine of objects in the same spot. The warm and busy interior that is not quite maximalist but definitely not minimalist.

It is not at all surprising to me that I am drawn to replicate Badgers Wood. It was a very happy home. For my first eleven years, my life was safe, loving and stable, yet adventurous. My mother, Chrissie, adored that house and she poured a lot of love and care into decorating it, looking after it and hosting in it. She could always be found working in the garden. It was a social home, too, with extra people often around the kitchen table and barbecues out the back, grown-ups lounging around, wine in hand, and kids running about in bathers.

The day we left, my mother had her first severe panic attack. Eleven years later (almost to the day), after many ups and downs, she died by suicide just as I was leaving home to make my way in the world. My childhood is neatly cut into two halves. The first half at Badgers Wood, with its stability and ease, and the second half, which included four house moves, my parents' divorce, my mother in and out of psychiatric hospitals and eventually her death just as I finished university. Because of this, I suspect I will never untangle homes from mental well-being; the two are linked inseparably in my mind.

Perhaps it is unsurprising, then, that I have a deep fascination with the decisions that go into creating a home. To find out more, I asked clinical psychologist Dr Emma Svanberg, who specialises in working with families, what benefits we might gain from exploring how our childhood affects our home environment as adults.

She explained to me that looking to our pasts, at where we come from and the things that have influenced us, can give us a depth of understanding about how we behave and feel today. Sometimes we can have very strong reactions to aesthetics, which can affect us very deeply. Memories can be unconsciously triggered by sensory cues. We might have an aversion to certain things and not understand why. Equally we may feel very drawn to certain aesthetics that create soothing feelings. Exploring how our childhood homes made us feel can help us pinpoint why we might be drawn to particular styles.

'So often', Emma says, 'not just in our homes but in life in general, we are focused on the external. What do we want something to look like? How do we want others to see it? What will others think?' But Emma tells me, in focusing on the internal instead, it can reveal a lot about how our homes make us feel and behave when we are in them.

'We have so many stories tied up in our homes, such as gender-based narratives around what it means about us if our homes are messy, for example,' Emma explains. Becoming aware of these stories can be really helpful in unpicking why we feel a particular need to have our homes decorated, organised or laid out in a certain way. It can also help us to think about how else we might like them to be. It's a way of approaching our homes from the inside out.

Emma talks me through an exercise that she uses with clients. She asks me if I would feel comfortable visualising my childhood home, and when I agree, she reminds me to tell her to stop at any time. Walking through a childhood home, even in your mind, can trigger childhood trauma and so she tells me that this exercise might not feel safe for everyone to do. I close my eyes and she asks me to visualise the home I associate most with my childhood, and when I do, she tells me to take notice of how I feel when I look at it.

Next, she asks me to walk into the kitchen. This room, she tells me, represents the heart of the home. She tells me to look around. 'Some people have a very strong visual memory of how things looked, and others may just get a feeling in their gut – either is fine.' She asks me to take a seat at the kitchen table or the counter and observe. 'Is it cluttered or pristine? Warm or cold? Can you smell cooking? Do you feel anxious or calm? Can you feel tension in your body?'

In my mind I walk to the kitchen counter at Badgers Wood and sit at a stool. Immediately I think of eating crumpets on cold winter mornings, of Mum buzzing around the kitchen, busy but always present. I see our dogs curled on the old sofa in the corner and think of how often I used to snuggle with them there; I see my brothers standing in front of the microwave making popcorn. I feel a yearning that I don't often allow myself to feel. Wanting something that is long gone, no longer accessible. Homesick for a home that no longer exists.

We repeat this exercise in the room she refers to as the 'nursery'. She tells me that this is 'any room you slept in as a child', and it represents our early relationships. Again, she asks me to sit down, look around and pay attention to how I physically respond to this space. What can I see and how does it make me feel? In my low-ceilinged attic bedroom, I feel comfort, not claustrophobia, in its tightness, like I'm in a cocoon.

I can see now how I have replicated the layout of my first kitchen in my current home, even mimicking the seat where my mother once sat at the table. I smile, thinking about how I turned my nose up at the idea of creating a large L-shaped open-plan ground floor when the builder suggested it. It's what many people do in 1930s terraces, he told me, in order to maximise light and space. But, no, I had recreated something much closer to my beloved childhood home. An eat-in kitchen with a separate living room. It just felt right, and still does.

Emma tells me that we can go through all the significant rooms in our childhood home in the same way, taking some time to observe and notice what comes up. They may not all be good memories, and she reminds me again that some people may not be able to do this without professional support. But it can be useful in identifying triggers, as well as the things we turn to in order to soothe us in our homes. When we understand where some of these aversions or needs come from, we can not only better meet our own needs as they are now, but also communicate them to other family members that we live with. Whether we are seeking something or avoiding it, our pasts often hold the key as to why.

We can also use a similar exercise to think about how we want to feel and behave in our homes right now. Emma recommends visualising yourself sitting in your favourite spot in your current home and taking the time to observe how you feel. What is the atmosphere like? Anxious, relaxed, playful? 'It's important to be honest,' Emma says. Then, as you walk around the home in your mind, she tells me you can begin to start seeing how you might be able to create more of the feelings and behaviours you do want in your home. It might be thinking about decoration that feels more fun, or finding ways to make it easier to get everyone to spend time together in one room. Whatever it is, the first step is just identifying what you want more of. This is a way that we can align our homes with our needs and values.

Homes that are built consciously around our values, that acknowledge our past, is another way of thinking about our spaces from the inside out. Rather than starting with the external – the colours, the layouts, the materials – we begin with how we want to feel and behave.

I think about the kind of values that Badgers Wood was built around. The land was bought by landscape designer Edna Walling in the 1920s. She had already built her own cottage there, Sonning, and when the land adjacent became available, fearing it would be bought by developers, she decided to buy it herself, becoming the first female property developer in Australia. The 18 acres were carved up and eventually sixteen cottages were built on the land. Local materials were used – rough-sawn timber, stone floors and walls – and saplings were cut down on site to create the pergolas that jutted out of the cottages. Edna believed that houses should be simple yet comfortable and that they should extend into the landscape. Dry-stone walls and terraces were some of her trademark ways to do this. She was one of the earliest garden designers in Australia using indigenous plants and by the middle of the twentieth century she had stopped using European plants altogether, as environmental conservation became more and more central to her work. Through her writing in books and magazines, she influenced the next generation of garden designers to look to the complex ecology of the Australian bush for inspiration and became a proponent for how residential areas can preserve the local ecology in a time when suburbs were expanding ruthlessly outwards. I grew up aware of this extraordinary woman who had built my home, although perhaps unaware of how unusual it was to live in such a place.

So how has this influenced the home I have created for my own children? I decided it was time that I took a deep dive into the past to find out. This would be my first time taking my daughter Agnes to Melbourne with me. Family travel has been mostly inaccessible to us due to my eldest son Arthur's disability. Ruairi, my boyfriend, was also coming with me for the first time. With Emma's words swirling around in my head, I knew it was time to revisit my childhood home, which I hadn't set foot in for three decades. Would it be as I remembered it?

When I lived at Badgers Wood in the 1980s, the street attracted those who were interested in Edna Walling's work, and we were surrounded by garden-loving families with kids my own age. Lucy, Emily, Georgina and I called ourselves the Bickleigh Brigade, and played in each other's gardens and houses as if they were our own.

Chapter One

To this day Lu, Em and Georgie are among my closest friends, despite the distance and the decades I have lived in London.

Emily's parents had been the last to depart the street, so she was my first port of call. Within twenty-four hours the old Bickleigh Vale network had worked its magic and I had the email of the current owner of my old home, Melissa, who emailed back immediately. Such is the nature of living in a home and garden that is protected by Heritage Victoria, interest in the house is not that unusual. She said she would be delighted to have us pop by and she was eager to hear more stories about the house. At the bottom of the email she wrote, 'I found this in the kitchen – I think it might have been left by your brother! I haven't wanted to get rid of it.' Attached was a picture of the inside of a pine tongue-and-groove cupboard. There were swirls of coloured marker in green, blue and pink, clearly left by small children, and in dark red, I could distinctly make out in a childish scrawl 'Ashley Wincer'. The cupboard was installed by my parents in 1981.

A few days before our visit to Bickleigh Vale, I sat around Lucy's table, all four of the Bickleigh Brigade together for the first time in five years, speculating over what I would find there.

Over coffee we all agreed that what we'd had was something extremely unique. To grow up in a mini paradise, in homes that reflected the natural landscape around us – it is impossible not to be impacted by that. Since those idyllic days we have experienced losses of all kinds. My mother's death, divorces, life-changing disabilities and illnesses. This shared village childhood, though, had given us a kind of bedrock that, looking back, we all agree shaped the adults we are now.

My friends' Bickleigh Vale homes had clearly influenced the aesthetics of their homes today, too. Lucy's home has echoes of our Edna Walling childhood throughout. A stone fireplace and natural materials, with views over densely packed gum trees and a large terrace with a pergola. It is a house that feels part of the nature that surrounds it and, we all agreed, the closest of all of us to what we grew up with. We talk about how comfortable we feel in this kind of house, even though circumstances have meant we don't all live this way. We are all used to smaller rooms, textured walls and stone terraces that invite the inside outwards.

They are all curious about what I will find at Badgers Wood, each of them with their own strong memories of the place. They, like me, cannot separate the house from my mother, Chrissie, who each of them were close to. As we drive away, Ruairi, who grew up in Northern Ireland, tells me he is more curious than ever to see this house, which lives so vividly in all our minds still.

The day arrives. The drive takes longer than I remember and we are a little late, but as soon as we hit Mooroolbark roundabout, muscle memory kicks in and I navigate my way to the street, pointing out where I used to go roller-skating and the local milk bar where I would spend my pocket money on a bag of lollies each Saturday. It is a flat, grey day as we drive past the endless streets of identical square houses with neatly mown lawns, privet hedges and two-car driveways. Tidy and suburban. Ruairi looks a little puzzled. It is not until we turn up Pembroke Road and slow down to look for the almost-hidden turning onto Bickleigh Vale that you can imagine what you will find there.

'Here we are,' I say to Agnes in the back seat, who pulls her earphones out and looks around. I drive very slowly, partly out of necessity (it's a single-lane road that is unpaved) and partly so I can drink it all in. It is much darker down this road, the towering gums and pines forming a thick canopy overhead.

Further up the road I pull the car in under a giant pine tree in front of my old front gate. As I get out I am hit by such a strong scent of home. Pine needles and eucalyptus and the late-summer flowers of the garden. It is unmistakeably the smell of Badgers Wood. The property has a dry-stone wall and white painted gate, just as it did in my childhood. The driveway slopes gently downwards away from the road, the house at the bottom. A dog barks and races up to greet us and we let ourselves in, closing the gate behind us. The garden looks a little overgrown, but otherwise nothing is out of place. The crab apple tree still sits at the top of the stone steps that lead down to the kitchen door. I think of the black-and-white photo I have of my mother standing in just this spot, back home on my bedroom wall in London. We descend the steps to the door, and I point out the windows above us. My old bedroom. Melissa opens the kitchen door, smiling, and ushers us into the kitchen to look around.

The first thing that strikes me is how right it feels. The kitchen layout is identical to how my parents built it, with an L-shaped worktop that looks towards the dining table and windows on two sides that look out over the garden. The freestanding cooker and the fridge have been replaced, but virtually everything else remains the same, including the kitchen units. I walk to the pantry; it is still the same. Melissa is just a few years older than me and within minutes we are talking about mutual friends. Melbourne, despite its population of four million, is a small world. She tells me that sometimes she will meet people and when she tells them where she lives, they remember being in the house when they were kids – childhood friends of my brothers. It is apparently a home that lives in the memories of many.

As we walk through the house, I point out the way we used to use the rooms. She is surprised to hear that what she thought was the formal sitting room was actually my dad's study, and the small room we watched TV in (we called it the den) is now a guest bedroom. I couldn't think of a nicer place to wake up, with windows on two sides of this small room, which makes you feel enveloped in the garden.

Upstairs, I show Agnes the tiny door to my bedroom. She is now the exact age I was when we moved out and she is a whole head taller than the door. She laughs as we push the door open and she sees how low the sloped ceilings are. She thought I had been joking when I told her I had slept in a room that grown-ups couldn't really enter. My brothers' rooms are unchanged, and again I'm struck by the 'right-sized' feel they have. They are small, designed for children and single beds, in keeping with the house's original feel. I think of all the house extensions I've seen as a photographer, where size has won out over design, our desire for 'bigger' trumping everything else. In my parents' old bedroom, I take a deep breath. It is just how I remember it. A box window above the bed and a balcony with French doors overlooking the gardens. And exactly, I now realise, how I have been mentally planning the loft room that I will eventually add to my house (one day, whenever I can afford to). Even my imaginary rooms are furnished by Badgers Wood.

Melissa adores the house and tells me the story of the day she first saw it and how she knew immediately that she had to live there. It feels good knowing she is the current custodian. She cares very deeply for it. When we leave, climbing back into the car, Ruairi turns to me. He tells me: 'I understand it all now. So much makes sense now I've seen it.' He means that I make sense, that my deep friendship with Lu, Em and Georgie makes sense, and that my interest in homes also makes sense.

*

South London

Back in London, I see my own home with new eyes. Reading again about Edna Walling and her aims for building the Bickleigh Vale cottages and gardens the way she did, I can see that I have replicated much of her ethos, without perhaps even being conscious of doing so.

The 1930s style of my house had appealed to me the moment I walked in when I viewed it. They are not houses that are particularly fashionable, Georgian, Victorian and Edwardian being the most coveted housing stock in London. But when I bought this place in 2012 I'd already spent years shooting in Victorian houses and I find them deeply impractical. They were built for a different age. One where servants or dailies came in to 'do' for you, so kitchens are dark and shoved in the basement or out the back, and indoor plumbing and central heating had to be retrofitted. Even expensive extensions are often left with dark, unusable dead space.

But post First World War life had changed dramatically, and families started living closer to how we do today, a fact that is reflected in the layout of the homes from that time. Four million houses were erected in the UK during the interwar period, and for many new homeowners, it was the first time they had plumbed-in bathrooms and electric kitchens. My house is a modest 75 square metres (about 800 square feet). We have one bathroom, three bedrooms (one of which is a small box room), a separate front room and an open-plan kitchen-diner at the back, which once upon a time had been a dining room and galley kitchen – I tore the wall out between them to make one larger room. The layout is so simple and well designed that every inch of the house is used. It feels spacious, despite its modest size, largely owing to the great light and the fact that I haven't packed it too tightly with furniture or kitchen units. It isn't very fancy, but it is beautiful in its simplicity.

With new eyes, I walk around the house. I see where I have unconsciously pulled influences from my first home. The balustrade that was sanded back and left raw rather than repainted. The whitewashed floorboards that leave the knots and patterns of the wood visible through the finish. The linen curtains and bedding that give a pleasing natural texture. The wood countertops, even though some kind of composite stone would be far more practical. The zinc-top kitchen table that reminds me of tin roofs. Even the pebble dash, which I love but is so hated by many that they have re-rendered their house exteriors flat and white. But I feel more at home with the rough texture and the natural colours of the pebble dash than I do with the stark, boxy coldness of a flat painted one. Now I think I understand why.

'Rather than a perfectly ordered and styled house, I find a kind of harmony in natural textures, colours and personal objects.'

I'm no minimalist, but having a disabled child who is prone to throwing and breaking things and is constantly engaged in some kind of messy sensory play has meant keeping rooms simple and not overstuffed. I prefer piles of books, double stacked on deep shelves, ordered only vaguely between fiction and non-fiction. I dislike bare countertops and enjoy seeing the silver salt pot that my parents were given when they got married next to the unbreakable enamel butter dish that was a gift to replace the many butter dishes my son has broken over the years. After some trial and error, most of the light fittings are now enamel, too. When I make my tea in the morning, I sit in the sun that streams in the back windows, on wooden chairs from Badgers Wood that anyone else might think don't 'match' the rest of the room. But I have never cared about matching things. Rather than a perfectly ordered and styled house, I find a kind of

harmony in natural textures, colours and personal objects. Perhaps it would be practical, given my son's needs, to keep the house completely streamlined and minimal, but the thought of living in a sterile space leaves me feeling cold.

These are all visual and tangible signals that I am 'home'. That my body can relax and be at rest. They speak to me like inaudible messages from the past, from my first childhood home when I felt safe and cared for. For others, those messages and cues will look different. And for others still, they may feel a deep need, whether conscious or not, to avoid feeling as they did in their early childhood homes and lean towards an aesthetic opposite. I can see now the benefit of being aware of where these inclinations come from, and why it's okay to embrace them head-on and accept why certain sensory cues will make us feel happy and safe and why some may make us physically recoil.

Though I am learning to embrace the echoes of my first home, I can see the dangers, too, in getting hung up on replicating something that is in the past. Four years after we left Badgers Wood, my parents were divorced, and my mother bought a different house back on Bickleigh Vale. Downderry is one of the most beautiful houses on the street. Painted pink and a ramble of interconnected rooms, it was a house that I had been in and out of throughout my childhood, and now it belonged to us. My mother was desperately trying to get back to a feeling of 'home' that had been lost. She bought it after the divorce settlement, filled with hope that going back to this street would save her. But it did not. She learned the hard way that there is no going back. The house and garden were too much work for someone as unwell as she was. Instead of a saviour, it became a millstone around her neck, reminding her constantly of a time that was long gone and would never return. A house, no matter how much you love it, does not solve mental anguish. Things only got worse, and this was the home I walked into after school each day, not knowing whether I would find her alive. We left after a couple of years, moving closer into town, to a smaller, much newer house that required less of her, with no old memories attached to it. In the small, secluded courtyard garden she built a patio of Castlemaine stone and brought a tiny piece of Edna Walling charm to the inner suburbs of Melbourne.

I like to think my mother would love my current home. That she would feel at home here. I have not been able to give my children the space and gardens and freedom that my parents gave me and my brothers, but then, so few parents can these days. But I hope I am giving my kids some of the things that my parents gave us. A home that feels safe and inviting, where friends are welcome. A home that is organised enough that you can go about your day with reasonable ease, but not so organised that you can't relax. A home filled with objects that are not necessarily expensive but are precious anyway. A home in which some care and attention to beauty has been given, but not so much that it stops you from enjoying being a child. A home that reflects our family values of being allowed to be our true selves inside these walls, even if that means it appears rough around the edges to others.

Chapter Two: The Big-enough Home

North Cornwall and South London

Size, for me, is a conundrum when it comes to thinking about homes. On the one hand it's what drives so many house moves and is possibly one of the biggest factors, aside from location, that most people consider when they are deciding if a house will become their home. And yet at the same time, there is often very little choice in the matter. As I write this, the average house price in the UK is nine times the average salary, and in my own London borough it is around 15 times the local median salary. Aside from friends who move across the country to less expensive areas, I personally don't know anyone who has much choice when it comes to size. You take what you can afford.

But as size and affordability is what drives so many people to move, it feels an impossible factor to ignore when thinking about homes. In a country with, on average, smaller homes than most of the rest of Europe, and with housing inflation sending us into what many experts are calling an affordability crisis, how do we decide how much space is enough? Is it possible that what is 'enough' is not quite as straightforward as 'more is always better', which can often be our default thinking?

North Cornwall

I had already shot Rebecca Proctor's home, just outside of Bude, Cornwall, for *Country Living* magazine a couple of years earlier when I got in touch to ask if she would chat with me about the decision to stay in their cottage as their children grew.

The small stone cottage sits back from the road, with the garden entirely in front of the house, surrounded by high stone walls. It is a lush and sheltered garden for this part of Cornwall, with its high winds. The cottage is low ceilinged and consists of two main rooms downstairs: a kitchen-dining room, the kitchen running along the back wall, with tiny windows overlooking a field beyond, and a separate living room, with windows to the front, overlooking the garden. Behind a small door in the centre of the kitchen is a set of

stairs that leads to the first floor. Upstairs, there is a double bedroom, the floor space of which is small, but with the ceiling removed and opened to the rafters, it feels airy. There are two single bedrooms, with specially built-in furniture handmade by Rebecca's husband, Andrew, a carpenter, and the family bathroom. The wall space above the staircase provides a library, and on the landing a compact desk creates an office. It is one of the most well-thought-out homes I have ever photographed.

Rebecca and I chat over Zoom, she in her pottery studio and me in my living room-cum-office.

'I don't actually think of our house as that small,' she tells me, and I agree with her. What I find interesting about her house is that, surrounded as she and her family are by space in the part of the country they live in, they use every bit of space available in their home. It is, in my mind, a right-sized house. Not luxuriating in space by any means, but all of it functioning, beautiful and suited to their needs.

And this brings me to a central question that I keep coming back to. How do we decide what is enough when size is a completely relative concept?

As is quite typical in Australia, I grew up in large houses. Badgers Wood, when I was brought home from the hospital, was a small two-bedroom cottage sitting in an acre of garden. When I was three years old, my parents had the money to renovate and we moved out for six months while the house was rebuilt, with the help of our architect neighbour and fellow Edna Walling enthusiast, Brian McKeever. It became a pretty large house at that point. Many (although not all) of my friends grew up in similar-sized houses, always detached and with a garden, on the outer edges of Melbourne where we lived.

My first experience of British housing was in 1985. My dad was working in London for four months and we all decamped there to be with him. The production company put us up in a Georgian terraced house and it was the first time I had ever been in a house taller than it was wide. From my bedroom in the basement, to my brothers' shared attic bedroom, I counted six storeys, although there was only one room on each floor. I'd never imagined houses like it existed before and we joked about not being able to tell which door was ours every time we walked home from school, from its rows of identical neighbours. When I returned home to Badgers Wood, my perspective had shifted. I ran around the house unable to believe how large it was. Had it always been this large? How can something so fixed – the size of a house – feel so completely different?

'A home will feel large or small, depending on your individual needs and your perspective, not because of square footage or the number of rooms.'

After a childhood of Australian-sized houses, I have spent my adulthood living in London, with a couple of years in New York – two cities not known for their generously sized properties. In my work I have been inside every kind of home you can imagine. My idea of what is small and what is large has adjusted and what I long ago realised was that using those words to describe a house is completely pointless. A home will feel large or small, depending on your individual needs and your perspective, not because of square footage or the number of rooms.

*

Since I bought my first flat, I have been quite obsessed with efficiency of space in homes. I was married at the time, and we made the choice to go as small, as cheap and as central as possible with our first flat, predicting (correctly) that we were at a point in our lives where size was not particularly important but later that might not be the case. The flat was less than 45 square metres (about 485 square feet) and had been built in the 1890s as a one-bedroom and converted into a very snug two-bedroom at some point in the 1980s. The bedrooms were so small that we had to search high and low to find a bed that would squash in, touching the walls on three sides. It was tiny and it was perfect. I also knew small would keep me from accumulating too much stuff, which, even in the days before Marie Kondo and the rise in popularity of minimalism in the mid-2010s, was something I was quite obsessed with. It was a hangover from moving countries a number of times in my early twenties, a whole lot of work travel and an urge to feel untethered by stuff. Flicking through old journals, I can see I also treated it as a sort of balancing act, trying to make up for the amount of flying I did for work by buying less stuff and trying to create less waste.

Efficiency of space and making do was already something I was practised at. From 2004 to 2008 we had lived in a one-room unconverted warehouse on an East London canal for unbelievably cheap rent. The ceilings were double height and the windows overlooking the canal were huge; I woke up each morning to the sound of ducks and geese and ripples of sunlight reflecting off the water. The price we paid for the cheap rent was no heating, having to install our own shower and kitchen, and sharing a communal toilet with the other live/work units on our floor. It was completely worth it, and I became incredibly good at coming up with solutions to the problems of stuff, storage and space. Mostly, it was a case of being discerning about what I allowed in through the door.

While working on shoots I was in Greek villas, French farmhouses and palatial London townhouses. But at home I kept my clothing strictly to a couple of drawers and one slim wardrobe. Our bed was a sleeping platform, and we made a headboard out of a low bookcase, so that I only had to roll over on my tummy to select a paperback to read in bed. I had discovered the joys and freedom of small living and no amount of shooting in large houses was going to sway me back. In the fancy houses I shot in, I saw debt, endless cleaning and repairs, and people shackled to high-paying, high-stress jobs. No, thank you.

The 45-square-metre flat lasted until we had two babies. I realised I had reached my absolute limit when I could barely get past my daughter's bassinet to climb into my own bed, and I had long ago lost the space for a desk to actually work at. I scoured blogs for small-living content, only to find that most people who wrote about living with less were downsizing to houses or flats around double the size of our current flat. Tiny was no longer the answer to my efficiency question. It was time to size up.

*

The average size of houses in any particular country changes slightly depending on how you calculate it. On the whole, the size of the average home in England and Wales is around 90 square metres (970 square feet), slightly smaller than in France, Germany and Italy (all 94 square metres/1,010 square feet), but bigger than in Ireland (81 square metres/870 square feet) and Romania (45 square metres/485 square feet). Over in the US, though, the average size is a whopping 245 square metres (2,640 square feet), while in Australia it's 186 square metres (2,000 square feet). This huge disparity in sizing across different countries means 'large' and 'small' means something different to all of us.

With the rising costs of housing and our need to change our consumption in the face of the climate crisis, how much space each of us needs is being reassessed by many. In the US, where average house sizes are among the world's highest, the Tiny House Movement has been gaining popularity. Defined as houses under 37 square metres (400 square feet), they are a reaction to the oversized, overconsumed modern American way of life and are designed to reduce environmental impact as well as living costs. Though this movement has spawned countless aesthetically pleasing social media accounts and a hit Netflix show, this is an extreme reaction, which does not, as yet, provide usable solutions to the average family in the UK who need an affordable home and want to consider their impact. In the UK, tiny homes can only be built on private land, out of sight, and so they are mostly used for weekend getaways and for people building them on private property belonging to family members. Although there are communities working to try to get sites up and running for collections of tiny houses, currently a tiny house is only a financially savvy way to live if someone gives you some land to stick it on. Perhaps it's unsurprising, though, that the Tiny House Movement has come out of the country that has the largest houses. A swing from one extreme to another.

Aside from the obvious privileges you would need to have for a tiny house here in the UK, is it really a workable solution to a housing crisis and overconsumption? Perhaps if you are a single person or a couple, it might be. But being forced to own a lot less stuff is not the only thing to consider in a tiny home. Privacy is another.

There is a lot of data to show that overcrowding can have a negative, lifelong impact on children. In England, a home is considered overcrowded if two adults who are not a couple have to share a bedroom and if two people aged ten to twenty, not of the same sex, have to share a room (two of the same sex sharing is okay). Children aged from one to ten of any sex can share a room, and babies under one don't count. There is also a minimum amount of space required in a bedroom for the number of people sleeping in it (children under ten count as half; all those above ten count as one person). Currently 3.1 per cent of households in England are classed as overcrowded, but that number jumps significantly for specific ethnic groups. Qualitative research shows that overcrowded households experience strained family relationships, increased stress, depression and anxiety, disrupted sleep patterns and, for children specifically, increased respiratory illnesses, increased mental illness, increased developmental delays and difficulties studying and completing homework. Clearly, 'tiny' is not the workable solution for everyone that many influencers think it is.

On the flip side, we have a tendency to think bigger is better when it comes to houses, but that's not always the case. Years ago, a client I was working with over a number of months moved out of her enormous semi-detached Victorian house and, not having found another in the neighbourhood that she and her partner wanted to move to, they decided to rent for six months while they looked. This same client was often envious of the houses we shot in and worried over not finding anything as big as they had previously owned. I remember clearly how surprised she was a few months later when life was actually easier for her in a moderately sized three-bedroom apartment with her husband and two young kids than it had been in her enormous five-bedroom villa. She had not realised how much time and energy such a large house was sucking out of her. I had not found myself desiring the lives of the homeowners whose houses we shot in, in the same way she had. What I saw was a huge amount of stress and the need for staff to keep everything clean and running as it should. A large house is not just expensive to buy, it's expensive and time-consuming to maintain. I always found it ironic that in these houses, the homeowners could afford to, and made the effort to make, more sustainable choices such as buying organic fruit and vegetables and using sustainably sourced materials, but the amount of energy it would take to keep the house at a comfortable temperature all year round for just a few people meant their environmental impact was enormous.

*

Rebecca and her husband, Andrew, bought their cottage in an almost derelict state 15 years ago, before they had children. She tells me it felt huge at the time, coming from an inner-city flat. They chose the house because it was exactly what they were looking for: a beautiful cottage, on their modest budget, that they could do up themselves. The previous owner was very elderly and had retreated to a single room, leaving the rest of the house to go into decline. Ivy had grown over the entire front of the house, the windows were rotten and the garden overgrown, but they could see the potential. The intention was not to create a 'forever' home, but to make something beautiful and see what life was like in Cornwall.

There was a time, she tells me, after the children were born, when she did wonder whether it might be time to move back to a city. Rebecca, who was a design writer and trend forecaster and continued doing that work on a freelance basis when she moved to Cornwall, had been missing the cultural and creative life of a larger city and easy train connection to other parts of the UK. But in the end the other aspects of life that Cornwall and the cottage offered won out and they decided to stay. It was then that Rebecca threw herself into her pottery business, which had begun at first as a creative outlet.

The house has evolved over the years to accommodate the family's needs. What had felt huge at first has had to shift and change with their family's growing needs. Andrew, an illustrator by trade, trained himself in joinery as they rebuilt the house and eventually started taking on commissions building bespoke wardrobes and bookcases for other locals. Andrew's love for the house, and for this part of Cornwall, was a great motivator to make the house continue to work for the family as it grew.

Their son Fred's tiny bedroom now has a purpose-built loft bed, giving him room to study and for his collections (Fred is an avid naturalist and animal lover). Their daughter Wren's room used to have a built-in cabin bed, which Andrew built when she was younger after Wren said she wanted to be able to have friends over to stay. He built it with both storage and a trundle bed that can be pulled out for sleepovers. Rebecca tells me, though, that it has recently evolved again. Older now, Wren wanted a bed that was easier to hang out on with friends, and the cabin bed was too high for that. So Andrew took away the lower storage and shifted the whole cabin to the wall where the window is, so that it's lower to the ground and the window opens in to the cabin bed. Rebecca tells me it has completely transformed the room, making it feel even more spacious and much more suited to Wren's needs as they are now. Really, she says, when you don't have a huge amount of space it is necessary to change it along with your needs.

In their own bedroom, Andrew removed the ceiling to create more of a feeling of space, and eventually, he did the same in Fred's room, allowing space for the loft bed. The landing originally was a reading nook, but that turned into the office as the family grew and Andrew built a library on the landing wall.

'It would probably be easier to live in a bigger house,' she admits with a laugh, 'and not be constantly changing all these things. But to be honest we do quite enjoy it. We like coming up with ideas and Andrew really enjoys the problem-solving aspect of carpentry.'

What appealed to me most when I walked into Rebecca and Andrew's cottage was how 'right' it felt. This is a house that has evolved over a

fifteen-year period to meet the needs of their family as they were at any given time. Some people might call it small, although Rebecca sees it as neither big nor small. For me, it's a home that evokes the concept of the 'not so big house' as described by architect and author Sarah Susanka.

Originally from England, Sarah had been a residential architect in the US for over a decade when she began to gather her thoughts around this concept. She could see all around her that houses in the US were continuing to grow in size, and clients often came to her complaining that they needed more space. But often, she found, what they needed was less but better designed space, rather than more rooms or square footage. She's clear, however, that this doesn't mean she thinks everyone should live in a tiny, or even small, house. A 'not so big house' is a house whose entirety is used every day. It is a house designed for the people who occupy it and for the life they lead, and doesn't contain dead, unused spaces.

She was noticing the growing trend of 'starter castles', or what we might now refer to as 'McMansions' – huge homes designed to impress rather than nurture. This impulse to buy or build big was based on outdated ideas about how we actually live now. So she set out to design houses that combined the beauty of a big house with the efficiency of a small house. She would reduce the square footage, but spend more per square footage, sticking with a client's original budget and producing something higher in quality and appropriate in quantity.

What I love about Sarah's philosophical and practical approach to home design is that it is not about dictating what sized home people should live in, but making sure the home matches the needs of those who live in it. When it comes to meeting the housing needs of a country that is facing a crisis in both supply and cost, this seems an extremely pragmatic approach.

Part of the reason why Rebecca and Andrew have never moved out of their cottage is, of course, the cost of housing in Cornwall. Cornwall has a large-scale housing crisis caused by multiple factors, including a huge number of second homes, lower wages than the average in England and industries that are seasonal. The housing crisis has a huge knock-on effect, making it hard to recruit key workers in the NHS and education, because of the challenges they face in finding somewhere affordable to live. Rebecca tells me that there have recently been some new homes built locally, which are only allowed to be sold as primary residencies. But they are mostly four-bedroom houses that are too expensive for local families to be able to afford, so they ended up all being sold to couples retiring from other parts of England. It begs the question: what's the point of building family-sized homes that families can't afford to live in?

*

South London

Back in Southeast London, not far from where I live, I arrive at the flat of fashion writer Alyson Walsh and her partner, Paul, who works for a housing charity. It is a handsome Art Deco-style structure, built over a number of years from the 1930s to the 1950s (the war putting a pause on construction for many years). Alyson's flat is on the top floor, accessed via an original lift, with large Bakelite buttons. The front door opens onto a long corridor that runs the length of the flat, which each of the rooms runs off, with windows facing the large communal gardens below and the London skyline beyond. The flat has two bedrooms, a bathroom, a kitchen and a living room, with a small balcony running between the living room and smaller second bedroom. It is neither large nor tiny, but perfectly formed, bright and well laid out. It is neither crammed with stuff, nor completely minimalist. I would call it considered and pared back, but certainly far from empty.

Alyson bought the flat on her own in 2000 when she became the fashion editor of *Good Housekeeping* and thought it would probably be sensible to get a mortgage while she had a 'proper' job. She had flatmates for a few years, helping to pay the mortgage, but then she could afford to live there alone and, eventually, Paul moved in and joined her there. It was a mess when she moved in, she tells me, but she was under the delusion that it would just take a few weeks to sort it out. She laughs at the memory. When she pulled up the old carpets she found the original lino floor. It's a rich burgundy brown, flecked with cream, and is beautiful. Around the walls are exposed pipes, the central heating for the entire building having been retrofitted. I quite like the industrial vibe. It feels truer, somehow, than boxing it all in and pretending it's not there.

Alyson is freelance now and mostly works from home, and Paul, like so many people, splits his time between the office and working from home. They had the second bedroom fitted with built-in ply wardrobes, which house Alyson's extensive collection of clothes. 'I can't wait to get rid of most of it,' she says with a laugh. But it's still too useful for her work for now, so although she keeps it as stripped back as possible, she needs a certain amount of storage for clothes. As well as writing for national papers, Alyson runs her own blog and social media channels, *That's Not My Age*, which focuses on fashion and beauty for older women. The second bedroom is her office, as well as her wardrobe and library of references.

Building storage into the second bedroom has freed up space in their own bedroom. The room is far from empty, with artworks, objects and a collection of shoes, but it feels airy and uncluttered, not stuffed with furniture. The long hallway that runs down the flat is lined with picture shelves and acts as a gallery. The picture shelves make it easy to change the display as often as they feel like it, and it regularly changes. Alyson laughs and says they have too many pictures, but by rotating them, you can enjoy them all. Once upon a time that hallway had been lined with low bookshelves instead, but she decided to get rid of all but her most loved books to free up the hallway.

In the living room, a 1960s dining table is covered in a bright African printed cloth. There is a green low-profile sofa, an Eames rocker and some mid-century patterned cushions. But the walls are white and there is very little artwork on them. A tall, wall-mounted floating bookcase houses Alyson and Paul's art-book collection.

'When the light comes in through the window in the evening, it hits the bookshelves and makes a beautiful pattern on the wall,' she tells me, 'so there is no point in putting artwork up there when the light creates so much interest anyway.' Across from the sofa is probably the most surprising item in their modestly sized flat. A large glass-and-metal display cabinet filled with every size of globe you can imagine.

When we think of small or modestly sized homes, we rarely think they might be places where someone can indulge in a collection. Yet, just like Rebecca and Andrew in Cornwall, Alyson is not what you would call a minimalist. She likes things. The globe collection began when Paul found her a beautiful antique one in Belgium. It became something they hunted down for fun as part of their travels. The collection has grown and spilled beyond the cabinet now into the bedroom. 'I suppose we'll have to stop,' she says with a laugh, 'but finding good ones is hard and expensive now anyway.'

'The size of the place means she has to think about what comes in, and also what must go out.'

Just like Rebecca, Alyson is considered about what she owns. The size of the place means she has to think about what comes in, and also what must go out. This matches her ethos as a fashion writer too. She believes in buying less and buying well and encourages her readers to find pieces they absolutely love and will hang on to. 'I've become an excellent style stalker,' she tells me, keeping her eyes peeled for key items each season.

I ask if she and Paul ever yearn for more space and she says no, the space is fine, but one day they might move, for a change of scene and a garden. They have been looking around Southeast London to see what might be possible. They may be able to trade in the flat for a small 1960s terraced house. 'But it will actually probably be slightly smaller in terms of floor space,' she says. Thinking more seriously about moving has also reminded them both of how much they love the flat. It really is pretty special, and they don't take it for granted. She feels very easy-going about whether or not they will decide to do it.

*

As I write this, I am awaiting news from my mortgage advisor. I am coming to the end of a fixed-term mortgage and it is about to go up by an eye-watering amount, the days of low interest rates long behind us. When I last took out a fixed-term mortgage five years ago, I thought I would be able to afford to borrow money to increase the size of our house round about now. But a pandemic affecting my income, the increased costs of living and the rise in interest rates (not to mention the hugely increased cost of building materials) mean that is definitely not happening anytime soon.

With two (almost) teens, having one bathroom is starting to become a cause of much arguing and stress. Our modest house was perfect for a young family. The kids were always under my feet anyway, we use every inch of it, and it doesn't take too long to clean. I never bemoaned the lack of a downstairs toilet, despite warnings from others with young kids. Nor did I ever have the urge to build an extension on the back – it would be hugely expensive, would ultimately ruin the current layout, creating dark or difficult-to-use spaces, and would only give me a bigger kitchen, which I don't really see the value in. But I have always planned on going up.

The level of noise in this space-efficient house has always been an issue, with my son's often sleepless nights combined with his inability to control the volume making it a little too easy for sound to travel. I have always dreamed of adding a loft room containing a master bedroom and bathroom. A space in the house to retreat to when it's noisy. It would free up a double bedroom on the first floor for my son and would mean that the box room, which he currently sleeps in, could become an office for me. We didn't need it when the kids were young, but I knew we would probably need it as they grew. I'm now starting to feel the pinch of the small house, even in the amount of room their clothes take up drying in the winter – so much bigger than the tiny little sleepsuits and cloth nappies of their early years. I don't need more space to fill with more stuff. But we all need a bit more privacy and quiet.

With the prospect of adding a loft room off the cards for at least the next few years, I settle down to watch *Tiny House Nation*, the American TV series, to see if I can get inspired by small living like I did in the old days when I went from a loft with a sleeping platform, to a teeny flat, to what felt like a palatial house by comparison. I want to get swept up in the cult of small and the romance of owning little and feeling free, just as I did back then. I curl up and watch episode after episode, sucked in by the usual emotional heartstring-pulling of reality TV. A family sell their house and go tiny to put their daughter through college. An older couple on a second marriage are evicted from their long-term rental and can't afford anything locally, so they go tiny instead. A young couple leaving their defence jobs are drawn by the lure of financial freedom that a tiny home can bring. I watch as the reality of how small their new homes are dawn on each of them, the TV-show hosts helping to make the spaces as efficient as possible, but also trying to help them understand the realities and sacrifices of living in a home the size of a trailer. I am swept away by their stories, excited by how thrilled they all are with their new homes. But I am also left feeling incredibly sad about the state of housing across the globe. That people must choose between homes and educating their children. That you can get turfed out of your rental home with sixty days' notice after fifteen years. While going tiny made sense for these particular people, most can't turn to tiny homes to answer these complex problems of inequality that our society faces, nor should they have to.

But after watching episode after episode of space-saving clever designs and delighted homeowners revelling in their newfound freedom, I am reminded of one thing: that size is completely relative, and our home is in fact a palace in comparison. I will not need to fold away my bed when I get up in the morning, nor will I have to tidy away my laptop before I serve dinner for the kids. My children don't have to share a bed with a relative and my daughter has a door she can shut on the whirlwind noise of her disabled brother and do her homework at her own desk, with her own things around her. We might not live in a very big home, but we do live in a big enough one.

Chapter Three: The Objects in Our Home

Bath and Flaxton, Yorkshire

Our homes are made up of not just the walls and roofs, windows and doors of the buildings themselves, but all the items we choose to bring into them. Home is in the furniture, the light fixtures, pillows and blankets, built-in cabinets and mirrors. From the intensely practical items in the kitchen and understairs cupboards to the more frivolous and decorative, we are surrounded by objects. Some will have been extremely intentional and others we'll be hard-pressed to remember where they came from. But how much of the way our home makes us feel is to do with the objects we collect, keep, discard, love and ignore on a daily basis?

Bath

It is midsummer's eve when I walk through the large glass doors of Berdoulat. It's a glass-fronted eighteenth-century shop in Margaret's Buildings, a beautiful pedestrian street in the World Heritage city of Bath. It has been many things over the years: a carriage maker's, a china warehouse, a cheese and wine merchant, and in 1889 it became Cater, Stoffell and Fortt, which sold high-class provisions to the well-heeled locals for over a hundred years. The shop I see before me now is the product of remodelling that happened in 1890. It has double-height ceilings to a galleried first floor, a mahogany counter and cabinetry that runs down one entire side and gold-leaf signage for 'High Class Tea Provisions'. Around me are beautiful, carefully selected homewares and provisions: wine, kitchenalia and crockery, Bath Oliver biscuits (which originated on this site), cookbooks, tea and more.

But the shop is not all that it seems. Behind a single closed door, the building continues, mirroring the shopfront almost exactly with a double-height galleried first floor and rooms beyond. Number 8, Margaret's Buildings is both a business and a home, occupying what was once three buildings, now joined together. I am here to visit Patrick and Neri Williams. Their company, Berdoulat, is both a shop and a design studio and it also happens to house their home, blurring the lines between public and private space.

I follow Patrick and Neri up a steep flight of stairs at the back of the shop to the first floor. We go through a tall, partially glazed door and into the first-floor gallery, one that had previously been hidden from view but which mirrors the public one at the front. Sunlight pours in through the large pitched skylight at its centre, and on the ground floor below us I can see the Williamses' kitchen. It is a magnificent space, lined with bookshelves and art, with an internal courtyard at one end and windows indicating rooms beyond at the other. We settle ourselves on the sofa in the gallery to chat. I'm eager to learn more about the building.

'In our design practice,' Patrick tells me, 'the building is the client.' They specialise in heritage buildings and do everything from total refurbishment to sourcing single items for both commercial and domestic spaces. He tells me it begins by listening to the building, a three-way conversation between it, the client and Patrick. Margaret's Buildings is the third family home they have made for themselves and their two daughters. Previously they lived in and ran a B&B, also in central Bath, and before that, they were in a former pub in Wapping, a historically industrial neighbourhood just past Tower Bridge in London. The objects they own, the art on the walls, all of it has been collected over time, but equally, each home has been different, and what has worked for each building has been different, too. It's a conversation that changes slightly with each move.

Neri points out the doors to the central courtyard. They bought them about twelve years ago in the South of France, falling in love with them and strapping them to the roof of the car to bring them back to England. The doors lived under their bed for a decade because they didn't have quite the right spot for them. When they designed this gallery space, finally they realised they had the perfect home for them. Patrick tells me he finds it so interesting when found objects then become part of the fabric of the building itself. When they move on one day – which they will, because they enjoy the process of refurbishing homes – the doors will stay behind. Patrick then points

to the partially glazed door via which we entered. He had it made to replicate the shape of the French doors, using the same dimensions and proportions. So those doors that they have loved and wanted to use for years have changed the building in multiple ways.

I ask them both if it's a challenge, finding homes for their furniture and objects when they move. Sometimes a piece of furniture or an object doesn't work anymore, they tell me. Patrick points to twin marble pillars that flank the bookcase in the gallery opposite us. 'They wouldn't work in a farmhouse, for instance. It just wouldn't feel right.' But mostly they have collected and hung on to their possessions over a long period of time.

'Objects retain more meaning the longer you hold on to them.'

'I've actually never really thought about it,' Patrick adds, 'but looking around, I don't see a single thing that we have just walked into a high-street shop and bought.' Everything is either antique or second hand, made by themselves for Berdoulat or made by friends who are artists. 'Objects retain more meaning the longer you hold on to them. When you move it's a bit like playing Tetris. Not just physically, but also emotionally.' Again, my thoughts drift back to the idea of a conversation between homeowner and building and objects.

In 2015 I finally made the decision to ship some of the belongings my mother left to me from Melbourne to London. They had been sitting in storage for the fifteen years since she died. In that time I had moved to London, to New York and then back to London again. I lived in shared houses and warehouses, and then my very first flat, which had been so tiny I couldn't fit any of it in. But in 2015, as a newly single parent to two small children, with moving back to Melbourne now off the cards indefinitely, I finally emptied that storage unit. I whittled it down to one pallet's worth of items to be shipped across the world. I chose four dining chairs, a Quaker-style armchair, some paintings, a few boxes of my mother's notebooks, photo albums and books, and another with some silverware and my grandmother's mid-century green-rimmed coffee cups. Not much, perhaps, from what had been a lifetime's worth of collected objects, but enough to feel my mother's presence in my London home. None of them are objects I would have chosen for myself. But they are all beautiful and somehow, as Patrick said, they have retained so much meaning over the years. I love the way they change the feel of my home by the way they interact with objects I have chosen, like different parts of myself on display. Emotional Tetris, as Patrick says.

Patrick's parents had both been schoolteachers and bought a ruined eighteenth-century farmhouse called Berdoulat in the South of France before he was born. The whole family would drive to France every school holiday and Patrick and his siblings spent their childhood helping his parents restore the dilapidated house, instilling in him a love and deep respect for old buildings. He also credits the experience, and his father particularly, with teaching him the art of curation – how a building, objects and art all work together to create something beautiful.

After studying fine art at university, Patrick worked and saved money for a few years to buy his first run-down flat. He spent each evening and weekend lovingly restoring it, and when it was done he decided he wanted to do it all over again. He soon started taking on design clients, and Berdoulat Studio was born. They started with an online shop first and then followed it a couple of years later with the physical shop in Margaret's Buildings The building itself and its history informed what they ended up selling in the shop. Wine, for instance, has a long history with the building, and though it had not seemed the obvious choice to add to an interiors shop, they decided it made sense.

Their previous home, run as a B&B, was created because they wanted people to experience what it was like to stay in a building restored by Berdoulat. Guests would often ask where they could get a teapot, or if they could purchase a chair, and this had Patrick and Neri considering retail for the first time. They decided, if they were going to open a shop, they wanted to create some of their own products, so that they weren't items you could get just anywhere. Simple classics that can be made in batches by local craftspeople, such as pepper mills, cutlery trays and candlesticks. 'Despite being made in batches, they are all entirely unique, by virtue of the fact that they are handmade and made from organic materials.'

Each Christmas Patrick's father, who became highly skilled at many crafts over the years, would design and make one object for each of the family members. A chopping board, a serving tray, a candlestick. Five versions of a single handmade object. A few of those designs have now been replicated and are sold by Berdoulat.

Patrick tells me the story of one of those objects, a magret board, which is a grooved carving board very common in the South of France, used to carve duck breast. He tells me: 'The interesting thing is, you can discern each of our characters by the way the boards have worn over time.' His brother's board is immaculate. He cleans it meticulously after each use and re-oils it regularly. Whereas Patrick says he often leaves his in a sink of water overnight, forgetting about it. It has knife marks all over it and a patina of use that has grown over time.

'Ultimately, interiors are portraits. They're made up of these elements that embody the people who put them together.'

'They have almost become portraits of each of us in the family,' he says.

It makes me think of my zinc-topped table, which holds the scars of a messy weaning baby, the outline of lemons abandoned during meals and splotches from the handicrafts of small children. Rather than bothering me, I love the way it tells the story of our family over time.

'Ultimately, interiors are portraits. They're made up of these elements that embody the people who put them together. It's like a private collection,' Patrick says.

He shows me around the rest of the house. Above the shop at the front part of the building is their bedroom, painted in green, a colour they created with Farrow & Ball, based on an original Georgian arsenic green colour they found inside one of the cupboards at 8 Margaret's Buildings. At the far end of the upper gallery is a long corridor that passes their youngest daughter Bonnie's bedroom and leads to a stairway downstairs. Past a tiny water closet (with a traditional flat-wooden-seated toilet), you arrive into the ground-floor living area, with another courtyard garden and the kitchen, which looks all the way up through the gallery space to the glass ceiling above. At the far end of the kitchen is the door that leads directly onto the shop floor. I can hear Neri's laughter as she chats to a customer, having been pulled away earlier.

I ask Patrick what it's like living in the shop. He tells me that being shopkeepers has made them part of the community in a way neither of them had quite expected. As well as homewares, they sell coffee and bread and baked goods, so they have got to know the local community really well. But it's also really lovely, he says, that on one side of the door he's selling a pepper mill and on the other, they're using it every day.

'It's not about dictating that you need to have this particular olive oil, or you must have this kind of bread knife. It's showing how everything we sell can exist within a context.' It feels right, he tells me, that they use what they sell.

The kitchen is split in two by a glazed, multi-pane wall, which houses the larder. It acts to separate the storage from the main eating area, but the room still retains a sense of space. Setting the larder behind glass immediately makes it feel less chaotic. Inside it, a dark pine storage unit runs along the wall, which has been part of the shop since the 1890s and would have served as storage for stock. The larder both contains and displays objects: cookbooks, candlesticks, crockery, tins of food, dry goods. It is a thing of beauty as much as it is practical.

At the centre of the kitchen is one of Patrick and Neri's dining-table designs. But it's not a showroom. This is a living, breathing family home, one that they welcome clients into and allow them to see in use. Patrick tells me the story of when they were on the hunt for a range cooker for their

previous home, the B&B (so how it functioned was really important). When they went to the range cooker showroom, they brought ingredients with them to cook a full English breakfast. He said the showroom let them do it because they were very lovely, but it was a pristine showroom, and no one had ever done that before. But how things function when they're in use is so important, and Patrick wants clients to feel they know how things are going to look, feel and function. Objects are the interplay between all these things.

In his book *The Language of Things*, Deyan Sudjic writes that 'Objects are a way in which we measure out the marking of our lives. They are what we use to define ourselves, to signal who we are, and who we are not.' Why else would we 'collect' things that we didn't need, and why else would luxury goods exist? (Sudjic suggests that collections represent a desire to impose order in an uncontrollable universe.) Objects go beyond form and function and, as Patrick tells me, come to create portraits of ourselves.

Not everyone inherits objects from their families. Nor may everyone want to. In Sudjic's book he recalls the politician Alan Clark's scathing description of fellow Tory minister Michael Heseltine as 'looking like the kind of man who had to buy his own furniture'. It reminds me of the scene from the 1985 Merchant Ivory film *A Room with a View*, in which Mrs Honeychurch, defending herself against aristocratic Cecil Vyse's snobbish view of her family, tells her daughter that they must put up with their slightly unfashionable furniture because that is what her husband bought for them and they are stuck with it. The Honeychurches are clearly not the kind of family that inherited their furniture. And sometimes what people value is something new, something that has never before been used by others and passed down. Newness often represents the ability to make your own choices, rather than take someone else's leftovers.

*

Flaxton, Yorkshire

Someone who I knew I wanted to speak to about objects is Kate
Sessions, founder of Sessions & Co., which bridges art, design and
interiors. Kate's background is in fine art and curation, but with
Sessions & Co., which commissions British artists to collaborate with
Kate on products for the home, she wanted to bring art into the
everyday. These are functional art products, designed to be enjoyed
by everyone, including children. Wall hangings that can also be a
baby play mat, cushions, mugs and quilts. Everyday items that can
be enjoyed for their utility and their beauty.

Kate and her family had recently left their East London home and
returned to Yorkshire, close to where she was born and raised, when
I emailed, so I didn't expect for her to be ready for me to nose
around her new home, but she immediately replied, telling me to
come on up for a visit. 'I haven't done a thing to it,' she told me;
'come see it anyway!'

Flaxton is a pretty, ancient village with a wide common running
down the centre of the main street. Kate's new home is a handsome
freestanding Georgian house, very different to the Victorian terrace
she left behind. Above the front door I notice a large white plastic
box, strapped down to the roof of the porch. Kate tells me they
recently discovered a beehive inside the walls and a local beekeeper
is luring them out and into the box. He'll take them away when they
have created a new queen. She laughs and tells me it's a bit of a
change from London.

'Kate's home, I realise, is in her
objects. The unique collection
of objects I associate with her.'

We walk through her new house, and I immediately get a sense that this is Kate's home. Where she belongs. I say so out loud, and Kate tells me I'm not the first visitor to say that. The funny thing is, Kate really has not done a single thing to the house. She has just moved all her stuff in. I recognise wall hangings, lampshades, cushions and curtains. Art is familiar, and so are the ceramics, the dining chairs and the mugs we sit down with for a cup of coffee. Kate's home, I realise, is in her objects. The unique collection of objects I associate with her.

We chat over lunch about her plans for the place. She tells me she's both excited to fix it up a bit, but also in no rush at all. The house belonged to the previous owners for a few decades, and over the previous twenty years or so the interior wasn't given much attention. It is in need of quite a lot of repair, and Kate and her husband are making the plans slowly. In the meantime, they are enjoying the feeling of knowing that this is exactly the home they want to be in.

She tells me that in many ways it's a relief to be here. Back in London, it wasn't unusual for someone to apologise for the fact that they had not yet renovated their house. A crazy thought, that people would feel the need to say sorry for not having the latest fashionable extension. Here, she tells me, it would not occur to anyone to do that. Your home is your home, not a showroom of the latest trends. She doesn't feel too attached to the plans for the house. If something happened tomorrow that meant they couldn't afford to do anything but the most basic repairs and updates, she tells me she's not sure she'd mind that much. It already feels like their home, worn carpets, peeling wallpaper and all.

The hallway is large and in the centre of the house, with rooms off to each side. It's a sea-green colour, with dark dusky-pink carpets and an original dark-wood curved balustrade. On the top-floor landing, curtains in Session & Co. fabric, which hung in her London home, flank the front window. They work perfectly in the space, as if they

were made for just this spot. The paint is peeling in places but there is a grand beauty to the place. The upstairs layout is unusual, with stairs here and there, leading to tucked-away rooms in a variety of colours and odd shapes. Her two eldest boys share a bedroom, and it's delightful to see the furniture and possessions I recognise from their London bedroom. Their room was always so magical.

'All the bedrooms have these huge cork boards in them,' Kate says with a laugh, showing me her own room at the front of the house, overlooking the common. '[The previous owners] had quite a few teenagers, I think.' The room is painted white, and it has indeed got a huge white painted cork board in it. I recognise the bedside light from her London bedroom, which they had an electrician install. There is no point waiting around for the day when they can do the place up. They just want to enjoy their own things in the house now, even if it means repacking everything up at some point. 'There is just no need to replace things or rush,' she tells me.

The move has also meant taking a pause in terms of designing new products for Sessions & Co. She tells me there is such a pressure to keep launching. But while she is taking the house slowly, she's taking the design process slowly, too – trying to avoid designing and pushing products just for the sake of forward movement, or growth for growth's sake. She's spending time developing new designs that are both affordable and flexible in how they're used. 'I want to really consider what is worth putting out into the world,' she says.

Though we might be accustomed now to conversations around fast fashion and the significant increase in the amount of clothes each of us purchases (approximately 60 per cent more items per year than we did fifteen years ago), fast homeware is an increasing problem, too. Commentators speculate that it's driven by a multitude of factors, including a higher percentage of renters than in previous generations, which makes purchasing small, portable items for their home, such as bed linen, cushions, vases and candles, an accessible way to personalise what can be a very impersonal space. Added to that is the fact that we now have a window into so many homes via Instagram. We have never before had so much access to the inside of private, often highly curated, domestic spaces. Like the amount of clothes hanging in our wardrobes, the expectation of what one might own continues to increase. As Alain de Botton writes in *Status Anxiety* (way back in 2004 before social media had taken over our lives), as humans we are not good at comparing ourselves to our historical counterparts (for whom life was full of deprivations), but we are excellent at comparing ourselves to our peers.

I have long acknowledged my own uncomfortable role in this cycle of consumption. As an interiors photographer, as well as doing editorial work for books and magazines, I also shot for commercial brands. It was my job to make lampshades, cushions and bed linen look as desirable as possible. Behind every shoot is a carefully constructed concept aimed at hitting just the right note with the target audience. Quite simply, my job was to make people want to buy stuff.

But I don't believe the answer is necessarily in rejecting consumption completely, only buying second hand, or getting rid of all our stuff and living with very little, as promoted by evangelical minimalists, counting out their meagre possessions in only double figures. Both of these stances are steeped in privileges that many do not have. And they are also lifestyles that are just not desirable for many. What we surround ourselves with, as so many people I have spoken to have said in various ways, is part of how we tell the story of who we are. It is how we feel safe. I think the answer is really much simpler and less extreme than total rejection. We could just think carefully about what we actually want and need.

Back at home, after my visits to Bath and Yorkshire, I walk through my own home looking at the items that I am most drawn to. The things I would save if I had to make some hard choices. My books, for a start. I have two alcoves of books, double stacked. Books, to me, are those funny, almost perfect objects, which contain multitudes. They are both representative of the content within and perhaps my state of mind when I read them, as well as a beautiful object. They exist in both the physical world and in my imagination, and they have altered me in ways that other objects do not.

I have a random collection of items given to me by clients over the years, sometimes in exchange for work. These are some of my favourite things, each one attached to a particular shoot and the person behind the brand, and often small luxuries that I wouldn't otherwise have been able to afford to purchase myself. And then there are plenty of inexpensive items, too, which I have become inextricably attached to. Things that have no value outside of this house, but which mean everything to me. The old pasta-sauce jar that I have kept sugar in for almost twenty years. It is worn, the lid battered, and each time I pick it up I feel deeply connected to the home it first appeared in – a very cold warehouse with huge windows overlooking the canal near Dalston between 2004 and 2008. I even love the cheap plastic soup ladle that I still use constantly, knowing that I bought it on a trip to the big Swedish retailer after I purchased my very first flat. These items would be meaningless to anyone else. But for me they contain the stories of my life, which far outstrip any external value that may be placed on them.

We need stuff. Each of us might need slightly different stuff, but there is a certain number of things that we need in order to go about our lives with some ease, safety and comfort. If an object is pleasing to use, makes our life easier or just functions really well, then those are excellent reasons to have it. But do we need endless amounts of stuff, changed and switched out to appease some kind of itching, uncomfortable feeling under our skin? Do we need to constantly update our stuff to stave off boredom? Perhaps not. Whether it's a new mug or an antique sideboard, perhaps how we should decide whether we need to acquire it should simply be based on a few questions, interrogating whether it would indeed make our lives a little better. Why does this make me happy? Does it function well? Will I use it? How many of these do I already own? Questions only we can answer for ourselves, that no stylist or influencer or brand can answer for us, no matter how desirable they make the object.

I think about Kate's new home in Flaxton and I wonder, if I upped sticks and moved to another house, somewhere completely different, could a friend walk into that new home and say, yes, this is Penny's house? Do the objects I own, love and use hold parts of me and, curated together, represent me in some way? I think perhaps they do. All the different identities I have held over a lifetime are represented in the multitude of objects I have collected over time. The paperback I read for a university exam. The mug my best friend gave me. The bed linen bought new when my marriage ended. I would still be me if I lost it all, but it feels good to look around me and see the stories of my life looking back at me – physical manifestations of a complex human life and all its ups and downs.

Chapter Four: Colour at Home

Barnet, London, and Stroud, Gloucestershire

I don't hold any particularly controversial opinions when it comes to home decoration. I have loved homes that are filled to the brim with different colours, just as I have loved entirely white ones. I don't live in an extremely colourful home, nor do I wear extremely colourful clothing, but I have always enjoyed passing through other people's homes that are colourful, just like I enjoy being in the presence of people who wear outrageously bright and bold clothing. I love wallpaper and lust after my own richly wallpapered room, but equally, I enjoy the calmness of a room not stuffed with pattern and stimulation. One thing I know for sure is that it has taken me time to understand that I have often held back in my own homes; that sometimes it is easier not to make a decision at all than to get overwhelmed with all the decisions we could be making about colour and pattern. I wanted to learn more about those who use colour confidently in their homes and whether this confidence was the key to bolder decision making. Is bolder always better?

Barnet, London

I had caught glimpses of author Huma Qureshi's home on Instagram before I saw it in person. I interviewed her and then we met in person at a literary event, and before long we realised we had a few strong interests in common: books, films and homes – a sweet triad of intersecting passions not shared by many other people we know. She was one of the first people I knew I must speak to as this book began to form in my mind. Someone else who understood deeply the connection between interiors and storytelling.

Huma's detached 1960s home, painted black with a mint-green door, sits at the top of a cul-de-sac and is an unintentional home in many ways. She and her husband, Richard, found the house online during lockdown while searching for a North London home for Huma's mother, who was planning to relocate from the Midlands. At the time they were living with their three young boys in Crouch End, in a small Victorian terrace. They had not intended to move. But it was the summer of 2020 and there was little to do and nowhere to go, so when the listing piqued Huma's interest, they decided to book a viewing just to satisfy her curiosity and get out of the house.

'I have always loved buildings and I'm fascinated by how other people live,' she tells me, as we sit down with coffee in her living room, where the picture window overlooks the front lawn and the quiet suburban street. It was the house itself that had drawn her in. Surprised and excited to find an untouched, freestanding 1960s home – an era of housing she has always loved – within London, she tells me she just had to see it.

Heavy social restrictions were still in place, so the boys sat out on the sun-bleached lawn while Huma and Richard took turns walking around the house with masks on. It was empty, the elderly owner having recently left to live with one of her children. The family bought the house off-plan in 1960 and it had been theirs ever since. It was virtually untouched from its original state and in need of a huge amount of love and investment.

'I've always loved what some people might call "ugly duckling" houses,' she says with a laugh – mid-century houses with amazing light and space but not much in the way of pretty decorative features. Crouch End, where they had been living, is wall-to-wall Victorian terraces, so when Huma saw the listing, not too far away in Barnet, she immediately sent it to Richard, almost as a joke at first. They put an offer in right away and it was accepted before they had even spent any time in the neighbourhood. The move was driven purely by the house.

'You know how people say a house has good bones? That's what it felt like. A house with good bones.'

The house is long, with the living room and snug facing the front, and almost the whole back of the house is taken up with a large open-plan kitchen, dining room and playroom. Double doors

separate the living room from the kitchen-diner, which, when standing wide open, give a double aspect and flood the house with light. It feels closer to the homes I recognise from my childhood in Australia, or California where my dad lived for a long time. It couldn't feel more different to a narrow London terrace.

The floors throughout most of the downstairs are yellow terrazzo, which feel cool underfoot. The kitchen is made up of three different colours of laminated ply in dark green, mustard yellow and a muted coral pink, with a chequerboard splashback in white and terracotta. Doors and skirting boards are painted in pale mint and baked terracotta, and arched glass doors lead to the back garden. Huma's office, tucked away on the other side of the kitchen, has wildflower wallpaper, a view over the garden and large-scale movie posters. Upstairs, a hallway runs down the centre with bedrooms and a bathroom to the left and right. It's wallpapered in a scalloped repeat pattern of blue, off-white and terracotta, and the floors are mint green. This is not your typical, tentatively decorated family home. There is a boldness, a confidence, yet a completely personal feeling to the space.

'The day we came to see it was scorching hot,' Huma tells me. 'I remember I walked in and it felt like houses we had stayed in on holiday in Denmark. These 1970s summerhouses. There was something about the light coming in on both sides that made me think of that and it has always stayed with me.'

'Huma tells me this house feels exactly how she wants home to feel.'

The design decisions that Huma and Richard have made have all come back to this. They wanted to capture the feeling of being on a summer holiday. She describes this to me as when you feel calm, happy and relaxed. She wanted the house to have a feeling reminiscent of good times, as well as to include design choices that felt right and appropriate for the building itself. Guests often comment when they arrive that it feels like a summerhouse, and she loves that other people instantly get it. Huma tells me this house feels exactly how she wants home to feel. Something that she didn't feel at their old home, even though they were very happy in that area.

I'm curious about the words Huma uses to describe the house – 'calm' and 'relaxed'. I could feel those things in the space, too, but I knew not everyone would necessarily use those words to describe a home that could count that many different colours in a single room. Huma tells me she regularly gets people online commenting that her home is extremely colourful, and she finds that interesting because she doesn't feel it's overly colourful at all. Yes, she tells me, she has used quite a few different colours, but they all have the muted feel of paint bleached by the midday sun, rather than being rich and saturated colours.

I was curious to learn more about each of our perceptions of colour when it comes to our homes. Why are some of us drawn to using a lot of colour, or particular colours? Why do others prefer almost no colour, or rely heavily on one colour, over and over? To understand this further, I got in touch with applied colour and design psychology specialist Karen Haller. Karen works with brands, interiors and designers to use colour for well-being and to create positive change. The answers to my questions, it turns out, are actually quite complex.

'A lot of interior designers say they prefer to work with a colour palette they like or are comfortable using,' Karen tells me, because while they love helping people create beautiful homes, they don't always want to spend the time 'getting involved' with peoples' emotions. This type of designer has their own signature style and makes adjustments to fit the client's lifestyle. This is understandable

in some ways, she says, firstly because it's time-consuming to start a design from scratch every time you work with a new client, but also because when people really open up, that line can get blurry, and an interior designer is not a therapist. Colour *is* emotion, she explains: 'When you work with colour, people can't help but emotionally respond.' So by avoiding colour conversations, the designer is avoiding that level of emotional response. There is another type of designer who works in a holistic way, creating schemes that are a true reflection of those living in the space – they embrace their clients' individual colour personality.

We are constantly responding to colour physically, mentally and emotionally, and are typically only consciously aware of it around 20 per cent of the time. It is woven into our emotional responses as well as our behaviour, and, as Karen writes in her book *The Little Book of Colour*, if we were to switch off colour, we would switch off our feelings.

So when it comes to making choices for ourselves in our own homes, does that explain why some people might be afraid to experiment with colour? Karen's answer to my question is interesting. It's less about not wanting to open ourselves up to our own emotions, she tells me, and more about worrying what other people will think.

Evolutionary psychology teaches us that because humans evolved to be completely reliant on the communities we live within for our survival (being cast out of a community would mean certain death), making choices that our social circles don't agree with feels extremely unsafe. In order to feel safe and accepted as humans, we have a tendency to make choices that the group will approve of. That tendency can mean that we find it easier to follow trends or make very safe choices when it comes to our homes. At some level, we all want to feel accepted, Karen tells me.

A study Karen carried out with a UK retailer found that 95 per cent of respondents were too nervous to go all out with colour in their homes, and 75 per cent decorated their homes to please other people rather than to please themselves.

Alongside this is something which a recent study by Annetta Grant at Bucknell University calls the 'market-reflected gaze' – a phenomenon whereby houses are becoming more and more similar due to fears that they won't sell on the open market if the space is too personal. Grant hypothesises that the rise in seeing our homes as a way to create wealth means there is conflict between what is a home and what is an investment, with the latter beginning to define interior aesthetics. Increased popularity of home-improvement TV shows is cited as one of the reasons for this. Basically, homes are getting less personal, blander and more boring.

But Karen is also clear to point out that just because someone is secure enough in themselves to decorate their home however they like, it doesn't always follow that a person will choose loud and bright colours. How we each respond to colour is so different, and lots of people love soft, quiet colours in a limited palette. Karen uses colour in her own home very deliberately but not necessarily in a loud way. When we feel comfortable in who we are, we can allow our homes to reflect ourselves, whether that be a riot of bright colour or something much more subdued.

It is our need to feel accepted and ultimately loved (the most basic of human psychological needs) that can drive us to ignore our own feelings and responses to certain colours and stimuli, and instead go with what society thinks we should want or need.

'Trends are something that are outside of ourselves,' she explains to me. If we are slavishly following trends, it's likely to mean we are looking outside of ourselves to feel accepted and a have sense of belonging. 'But that kind of external validation will never truly satisfy us,' Karen emphasises. 'To feel satisfied, we will constantly need to be looking outwards for the next thing, constantly pivoting and changing. This isn't healthy and can lead to a lot of emotional distress.'

Instead, we can look inwards and pay attention to how we feel and respond to colour. This, like so many habits, may take practice, especially for people who are used to ignoring their own responses. Pause and notice how something makes you feel and more importantly, your response, your behaviour. Karen says you may hear yourself making qualifying statements such as, I really like that colour, but … and we should pay attention to the but in that sentence. But it's too girly? Too brash? Too boring? Are those your thoughts or the thoughts of the culture around you that you have absorbed?

To illustrate her point, Karen tells me the story of an interaction she witnessed about ten years ago. She was at Portobello Market in Notting Hill when she saw a small girl excitedly rifling through a rack of colourful dresses. Eventually she pulled one off the rack and said, 'Mummy, I want this one!' and immediately her mother responded by saying, 'No, you don't like that colour.' Karen says her heart sank watching in real time as this young girl learned to doubt her own reactions. Over the course of a lifetime, we can absorb so many moments like these that take us away from trusting our own instincts and instead learn to copy the tastes of our social circles.

Trends can come about for so many reasons, including responses to large cultural events, and are often cyclical. Recently, maximalism has been big in interiors, with bold blocks of colour and lots of pattern. Karen explains that she is certain this is a response to lockdown, when we were all under-stimulated. I reminisce about the time twenty years ago when every single location house I shot in was white. Karen laughs, she remembers that time, too. We talk about the Elephant's Breath moment that happened about ten years ago – the

warm, mid-grey paint colour from Farrow & Ball that appeared in an impossible number of middle-class homes across the country. I ask her about the downstairs-loo phenomenon. We are both Australian and find the trend of having a downstairs loo wallpapered in maximalist styles and colours extremely British and funny. Karen's theory is that many British homes are very restrained in their style, so it's a way of letting loose in a socially acceptable manner.

This conversation about trends has come up a lot with homeowners that I have visited. Those of us who, for professional reasons, are in other people's homes a lot are noticing that creeping sameness mentioned earlier. Social media has given us all a window into so many homes, but like the idea of the 'market-reflected gaze', which may come from a saturation of home-improvement TV programmes, being exposed to so many people's homes online may actually be making all our homes more similar rather than more diverse. Our need to have 'Insta-worthy' interiors as a means of external validation comes back to the idea Karen mentioned as something that will ultimately never satisfy us. We will always be chasing it.

*

According to Karen, her theory is there are three main ways we relate to colour: personally, culturally and psychologically. The personal response is affected by our memories and individual history, such as our favourite sports team or our grandmother's wallpaper when we were a kid, much like the ideas I discussed with Dr Emma Svanberg in Chapter 1 (see page 24). The cultural is usually deeply embedded within our social culture, such as wearing black to a funeral in the UK, or a bride getting married in red in China. And the psychological is the emotional responses, which are largely unconscious and influence how we think, feel and behave without us even being aware of it. How we each respond to colour can be one or a mix of two of these, with the addition of the context of any given moment and how we are feeling at that time.

Karen gives the example of when someone is feeling really tired; perhaps they might put on a red jumper, knowing that red is an energetic colour that may give them a boost psychologically. One day that might work well, and on another, you may be so tired that the red is overstimulating, and you now find it draining. Context is really important, which is why, she tells me, it's useless and even damaging to think that we have just one response to every colour, such as *yellow will always make you happy* or *all greens are calming*. All colours have positive and adverse psychological traits and how you will respond will depend on the context, the colour and its saturation, proportion and placement as well as our personal and cultural associations.

This reminds me of a story that Patrick Williams, one of the owners of Berdoulat in Bath (see Chapter 3), told me. His father recently died, and he was told that dreadful news in the family room of a hospital that was painted entirely in what he described as an awful buttery yellow. He wondered aloud at who made that decision and why on earth they thought it was a good idea. Karen sighs and tells me this is the kind of thing that happens when people google colour psychology.

'Forget worrying about any kind of colour rules and simply pay close attention to how colours make you feel.'

This brings me back to what seems to be key. Forget worrying about any kind of colour rules and simply pay close attention to how colours make you feel. Colours might have some innate psychological properties, but the positive and negative effects of these properties are complex, so we need to learn to pay attention to how *we* feel and respond to them.

There are a few things, though, that we can all learn about the basics of colour psychology which Karen shared with me. Saturated colours, as a general rule, are more emotionally stimulating. While we may not be certain whether we will respond to a colour's positive or adverse traits on any given day (depending on context), a good rule of thumb is to observe your own responses on the amount of colour used, as this is personal to everyone. More is not necessarily always better. And we also respond more positively to colour combinations that are in harmony like we see in nature. We may not be consciously aware of disharmony in colour combinations, but we can often feel it if we pay attention. Something might feel jarring or off and we can't put our finger on what it is.

So aside from paying attention to how we respond to colour, how else can we make colour choices that help us feel and behave in positive ways in our homes?

Karen explained to me that alongside colour psychology theory, there is colour harmony theory which suggests that all of nature's colours can be categorised by the seasonal year. Each season has an energy, and we as human beings have a predominant season which is reflected in the colour palette. Spring colours are warm yellow-based, bright and bouncy and have vitality. Summer colours are cool blue-based, have a hint of grey in them and are serene and soft. Autumn colours are warm yellow-based, rich and earthy, with a little black in them. Winter colours are clear, cool blue-based and intense. Each of these groups of colours are in harmony with the other colours within the same group. And yes, each group contains reds, purples, blues, yellows, greens – just different tints, tones or shades. No colours are off limits to any person, other than black which sits in the winter colour group. I may not be a Barbie-pink kind of person, but I love a warm, earthy coral pink, for example.

Figuring out your predominant season can be a great way to begin to understand what colours might work in harmony for you. I took the quiz in Karen's book and was unsurprised to find that my primary personality came out loud and clear as an autumn, which I already instinctively knew. While seasonal colours are a psychological theory, there is a lot of experiential data to support it. But once again, Karen emphasises the importance of paying close attention to our own responses and physiological changes and listening to them above everything else.

This all makes a lot of sense to me and backs up how I chose the homeowners to interview for this book. I was adamant from the beginning that I was not interested in one particular aesthetic style. How I made my choices were based on how in touch I felt the homeowner was with how they wanted to live and the personal choices they have made within the circumstances they find themselves in. They are all people who pay attention to how they respond to the aesthetics that surround them.

Huma describes herself as an emotional person. She listens to how she feels – something that is not only clear in her home, but in the pages of the books she writes, which are about intimate relationships of all kinds.

But how do we learn to tap into this? We are not all raised to feel freely able to access our emotional responses and safely pay attention to them. I pose this question to Karen and ask, could it simply be a matter of practice? And Karen confirms that yes, it is and the willingness to connect from within.

*

Stroud, Gloucestershire

I drive west one morning to the market town of Stroud in Gloucestershire, where I have arranged to visit the home of Alice Begg and Robbie Humphries. I don't know exactly what to expect. All I know is that I have seen snippets and small corners of the

fashion and textile designers' home, and I am deeply intrigued. The house is Victorian, and the front door is straight onto the pavement in a way that, as an Australian, I still find surprising. The drive in from the motorway was stunning, twisting and turning along roads arched over with trees. It's one of those glorious midsummer days and the view over the lush valley and into the centre of Stroud reminds me why I live in England. The glossy red door opens and Alice shows me in. It's a steep house, built on the hillside for railway workers in the later part of the nineteenth century. At street level there is a living room, then down a steep staircase is the kitchen, the laundry and a bright, wood-framed extension. Up some more steep steps, on the first floor, is their daughter's bedroom and the bathroom, and up again is Alice and Robbie's bedroom, with dormer windows looking out to the street at the front and at the back to the valley below. A tall and narrow house, neatly stacked almost one room on top of the other. It's delightful and colourful and each room is a surprise.

Down in the kitchen, Robbie fixes us grilled cheese sandwiches as we chat. Alice and Robbie own Humphries & Begg, a fashion and homeware brand, which they began together as a side hustle just three months after they met in 2010. It began with men's suits and shirts in colourful Indian block prints, which took off when they were featured early on in *The Times*. Alice, meanwhile, had been running her own swimwear label, and when she decided it was time to let that go in 2016, she put her energy into Humphries & Begg full time, and the brand as it is now was born. They make clothing, accessories and homeware in Alice's signature patterns and bold colours. This is all brought to life in Jaipur, India, by Atal Abhay, in his family-run print and production house, which includes block printers, screen printers, tailors and seamstresses.

Alice, who studied art at Falmouth and fashion at Middlesex, knew from the beginning that she was not interested in designing within the traditional fashion industry. Her designs begin life as watercolour paintings, often at her kitchen table or while on holiday, where she takes inspiration from everyday life. She then creates repeat patterns digitally. Her fabrics have a hand-painted quality to them, and the colours are contrasting and bold. They are clothes and homeware that start conversations. Robbie, who is currently designing a new range of men's tailoring, tells me that when he wears one of his jackets out, people smile and often stop to chat to him. People might be nervous of wearing something that is such a talking point, but when they try it, he tells me, many people discover how much it makes other people happy.

Their home certainly makes me smile. The kitchen cabinets, which were found on Facebook Marketplace for next to nothing, are painted a bold Wedgwood blue on the lower cabinets and a dusky pink on the upper-wall cabinets. The wall behind the sink is a rich, saturated green, underscored by a splashback of handmade tiles with Alice's signature hand-painted brush-stroke patterns in pale pink, green and yellow. I ask Alice if she's planning to add the tiles to her range at Humphries & Begg, and she laughs. 'They took me six months to make by hand, so I don't think it would be commercially viable!' The whole room was put together by themselves with a little help from a friend who is a joiner, on an extremely tight budget. It is a joyful space, which can only be described as colour confident.

Upstairs, the living room is an intense, warm pink and the blue fireplace has been hand-decorated by Alice, with gold and pink repeat patterns. Alice shrugs and smiles and tells me she couldn't help herself. The family bathroom is tiled in pink and orange, perfectly in harmony with the blinds made from one of Alice's most popular fabrics, called Row of Soldiers, in pink, ochre and turquoise, with a matching hand-painted pattern on the plain white sink. At the top of the house, the sloped ceiling of the bedroom is painted a soft pale pink, with the pattern confined to the bedhead (again, hand-painted by Alice) and the bedding and lampshades from ranges they sell at Humphries & Begg. The main focus of the room is the large triangular window, which gives a stunning view over green treetops.

'But that is exactly what makes
a home, a home. It's for them,
not for everyone.'

What strikes me most about this lovingly handmade home is the
confidence with which Alice and Robbie have made it their own.
It is the exact opposite of the 'market-reflected gaze'. It is deeply
personal, experimental and joyful. It's also not for everyone; some
would find the saturated colours and use of pattern a bit
overstimulating to live with all the time. But that is exactly what
makes a home, a home. It's for them, *not* for everyone.

What I see playing out in Alice and Robbie's home is Karen's advice
to practise noticing and listening to our aesthetic responses. Alice has
had a lot of experience, from art school through to her career as a
designer, in playing with colour and pattern and learning what she
positively responds to and what she doesn't. Like Huma, she has the
confidence to have a kitchen in multiple colours, not because they are
following a current maximalist trend, but because they both pay close
attention to how colour makes them feel. Both homes are inward
looking, reflecting the personal needs and desires of the families who
live within them. It's a feeling that is instantly apparent when you
enter them both, in the same way that I can feel it when I walk into
a home that is decorated based on surface trends and values external
to the homeowner.

For those who haven't spent their lives and careers paying close
attention to how colour and pattern make them feel, where do they
begin? I pose this question to Karen and she quickly tells me it's not
about spending money. It begins with play. 'Start by looking for the
things hidden away in cupboards,' she says. People are often
surprised by the objects they already have. Try placing collections of
objects around your home. Move things from one room to another.
Leave it there for a few days and see how it feels. Karen is also a big

fan of charity shops for playing with colour. 'We can't all be consuming all the time, it's just not sustainable. Charity shops, junk shops, are a great way to experiment. Buy vases, jugs, cushion covers in colours you are drawn to.' It's a low-stakes way to just play with colour, with no pressure to get it 'right', which you might feel if you attempted to paint a whole room. Karen is also a big fan of decorating with flowers, fruit and vegetables. Cut flowers from your garden or put big bowls of fruit and vegetables out that you'll eat anyway. This kind of colour injection can go a long way.

In my kitchen, I think about how I have applied this idea. Behind my sink is a windowsill, which is the only safe place in my house to have indoor plants (my son loves to dig into soil, so I can't have plants anywhere else). I think about why this makes me feel so happy every time I see the view of it as I walk through the front door. It's the combination of rich green leaves of herbs in their terracotta pots, which softens the hard edges of that white wall and window frame. It's a cheap and pleasing way to inject some colour and texture into what could be a cold area of the kitchen. Using colour in the home is not all about major redecorating projects. It's mostly about noticing and giving ourselves permission to play.

In the light-filled, wood-framed extension off Alice and Robbie's kitchen, I spot their daughter Honey's dolls' house. Robbie tells me they found it cheap on Facebook Marketplace and the two of them set about fixing it up for her for Christmas. It's a three-storey Victorian home with a front

porch and gabled windows, and a shingled roof, which they made themselves. They have painted the exterior pale lemon yellow, with a blue trim, complete with a blue repeat pattern around all the windows and framework. Robbie pulls it out and turns it around for me to see. Inside are curtains and rugs made out of their own bright fabrics. They collected cheap wood dolls' furniture from car boot sales and painted the rooms in pink, turquoise and blue, with hand-painted patterns and miniature artworks printed and hung on the walls. It might just be the most delightful dolls' house I have ever seen (and I once had the lucky job of photographing one that cost upwards of £20,000). It is the epitome of playfulness.

As I wave goodbye to them, carrying a gorgeous purple-and-blue patterned jumpsuit that Alice has pushed into my hands, insisting I take it with me, I vow that I will allow myself to experiment more with my home. I will pause and notice more. I will pay attention to how different colours make me feel at different times. And I will play.

Chapter Five: A Home of One's Own

Waltham Forest, London, and Northumberland

Chapter Five

One of the things that has become more apparent to me over the years is how much having my own home gives me a small sense of control. When caring, disability, single parenthood and freelancing means that I sometimes feel at the mercy of every blip in the economy and every whim of the government to give and take away as they please, my home has been a constant. It has been a small haven in which I feel like I'm the one in charge. That comes with responsibilities, of course, but it also comes with a freedom that I don't always feel in other areas of my life. Homes are so much more than a place to lay our heads. They are a small world from which we launch ourselves into the universe each day. When they are safe and feel like they are our own, everything else feels more possible. Sometimes what we need when life is challenging is a safe place where we can exert some control.

Waltham Forest, London

I drive down a wide tree-lined street in the East London borough of Waltham Forest, blossom falling like rain drops on my car. It's a beautiful day, sunny and mild, after a dull grey spring so far. Emily Wheeler meets me at the entrance to the non-descript low-rise council flats and shows me upstairs. The work she and her team have been doing on the flat was only finished late the night before and, for safeguarding reasons, I have had to come and shoot it before any of her client's personal belongings have been unpacked and are visible.

As I walk into the lounge I actually gasp, such is the contrast with the flat, grey exterior. Sun is streaming in through the bay window, outside of which the view is entirely of the tops of cherry trees. It is a serenely pretty space, small but bright, with a round table and two chairs under the window and a gorgeous plump sofa. Unlike most of the houses I have shot in my career, every single thing in this flat is brand new, from the crockery set out on the table to the art on the walls. The woman this flat belongs to has lost everything and this is her chance to start again.

Everything has been thought of, from mirrors and artwork, to cosy throws and rugs. I ask what the client's reaction was when she came home the night before, to see it fully furnished and styled for the first time. Emily says she was quite overwhelmed. Even though she has made a lot of the choices herself (all the pieces of furniture, for example, have been chosen by her), seeing it all together, Emily says, is often a very unexpected experience for the client. The care and attention to detail that is put in to finishing their flat by Emily and her team is often of a kind that they are not used to receiving.

Emily, founder of the charity Furnishing Futures, began her career working in child protection. It was work she was deeply passionate about, but it was also extremely difficult and, like so many social workers, by the time she was in a senior position, she'd had some experiences that had made her feel very unsafe, she was burnt out and she needed to take a break. She decided to retrain as an interior designer, and afterwards ended up getting into freelance interior styling and writing for magazines. Emily was a parent by this stage and as her family grew and they needed to buy a home of their own, it made sense to return to social work and become the family's breadwinner again. She was glad to be back doing work that was deeply fulfilling, and her two different career experiences had given Emily a unique insight.

During all the years that Emily worked with vulnerable families, it became clear to her that not only was having a safe, clean and warm home vital for well-being, but that furniture poverty had a huge impact on childhood development. Families fleeing domestic violence and leaving without a stitch of clothing other than what they are wearing that day, let alone any furniture, might be given emergency housing, but those houses are rarely adequately furnished. And if you are lucky enough to finally make it to more permanent social housing, it comes completely bare, with no flooring, no curtains, no light fittings or white goods. Emily told me that while once upon a time councils may have helped link up residents with charities who could provide some essentials, after thirteen years of the Conservative government and a cost-of-living crisis, most of those initiatives were either gone or massively oversubscribed. If you are lucky, she told me, you might get help with a few of the larger basics, such as a washing machine and a cot for your baby.

'A place to live, though vital, is not enough. It needs to feel like a home.'

It was clear to Emily when she visited homes that this was having an enormous impact on families that had already experienced trauma. Babies who don't learn to crawl because the floor is cold, hard concrete. Primary-school children who struggle to learn because they are sleeping on a hard floor. Teenagers with no desks or privacy to study. Mothers who cannot relax in their own homes, unable to process the trauma they have been through. A place to live, though vital, is not enough. It needs to feel like a home.

At the same time, Emily had seen the amount of waste happening in the interiors industry. There was a huge amount of perfectly good, brand-new furniture and accessories going to waste, being dumped in landfill, largely driven by customer returns, minor damage and out-of-season stock. The cost of storing this furniture is enormous and brands are desperate to get rid of it.

'No one should be living in furniture poverty,' she told me. There is enough furniture out there, so no one should ever need to go without.

It was during this time that Emily and her husband bought their own home. With no money left to speak of, and having grown up with a mother who bought and sold vintage furniture, Emily went about filling up their first home with cheap and free items she found on Facebook Marketplace. As she drove around her London neighbourhood, picking up gorgeous bargains that others didn't need anymore, she began to think about the families she was seeing at work and wondered if there wasn't some way she could do this for them.

Emily knew that it would be hard to help many people if she could only track down a single item at a time. These families needed everything. If you have nowhere to wash your children's clothes or refrigerate and cook their food, if you have to put your children to sleep on a floor each night, or on bare mattresses with no bedding, the likelihood of returning to a dangerous situation is very high. And it is in returning that women are at their most vulnerable to violence.

As well as the essentials, Emily tells me, what these people need is a chance to exert some control over their space, make choices about how they want their home to look and feel, after they have lost so much. After the strength it has taken to leave, they shouldn't have to feel as though they are begging for bits and pieces to make do. And so the seeds for Furnishing Futures were sown.

In a very short space of time, the project has grown from Emily's side hustle to a fully-fledged charity. Women are referred by a few domestic violence services and Furnishing Futures works with the beneficiaries to completely design, redecorate and furnish their new

homes. For those in temporary and emergency housing, they help with essential items to tide them over until they are in a more permanent home. The furniture is largely donated by interior brand partners, who deliver brand-new stock to Furnishing Futures' East London warehouse – everything from beds and sofas to kitchen handles, lighting and cushions.

Inside the Waltham Forest flat, Emily and the designer, Ruth Milne, who has volunteered on this particular project, show me around. The client who lives here, whose name I am never told for safeguarding reasons, chose the colour scheme. The design team put some ideas together, based on her likes and dislikes, and then items were pulled together in the warehouse for her to look through. Anything that was missing that she needed was requested from brands or bought from the charity's funds. They do their best, Emily tells me, to involve the client in the process as much as possible, just as you would a paying client. They are there to advise and guide, but not to tell the client what they should or shouldn't have. There are some restrictions, such as access (width of stairs, availability of lifts etc), flooring requirements for certain buildings and being able to get hold of the right furniture, but they work together to make the home meet the client's needs and hopes.

The charity faces many unique challenges. Having enough storage to take donations (this is a lot more storage than you would think, as brands are often unwilling to donate unless they can send large quantities), as well as all the logistics of moving furniture, laying floors, painting and decorating, all while working with vulnerable women who have experienced trauma.

They have done the hardest thing, Emily tells me. They've escaped really difficult circumstances, and they have a chance to start again. But they're also dealing with the legacy of that trauma and caring for children who have also experienced trauma. It means that Emily can't allow any tradesmen or interior designers to be in the flats if the client is there. She is now inundated with people wanting to volunteer their time, offering to help with the design and implementation of the work, but Emily is not able to outsource most of this work as yet. Making sure clients feel safe is her number-one concern, so being trained in safeguarding and being trauma informed is absolutely crucial to the process. Imagine if you had experienced violence in your own home and then came back to your new flat one day to see a strange man installing a curtain rail? It just can't happen like that, she tells me.

We drive fifteen minutes to the charity's huge, airy warehouse, which holds their offices as well as storage space for donations. Eventually, Emily wants women to be able to walk in here and choose furniture and accessories as they would in a large shop. No one likes to feel as though they are being given someone else's leftovers. The way the women experience the service is as important to her as the end result. There are many plans to expand. Emily is currently in the process of hiring an operations manager. Next, she'll be looking to employ another social worker. After that, she would love to employ her own small team of installers. In an ideal world, it would be an all-female installation team. The thought of Emily employing a team of trauma-informed tradeswomen makes me smile. And her larger goal? For the charity to create a replicable model and spread around the country, so that no matter where someone lives, they can be referred to their services. That, and keeping as much furniture out of landfill as possible and putting it into the hands of those who need it most.

It becomes clear as Emily and I chat that although her job is to create beautiful flats, that's actually only a small portion of what she is doing. She is giving these women a tiny bit of control over their environment, after they have spent years – in some cases a lifetime – having that taken away from them.

Decorating a home is not a surface-level thing. It's about truly occupying the space. Allowing it to reflect your own needs, desires, interests and joys. Simply tossing a person a set of keys to a secure flat is not enough to make them feel safe. Many times, Emily has seen how families she has worked with as a social worker have remained on intense high alert, unable to relax even when technically they are safe. But as Dr Emma Svanberg told me when we spoke (see page 24), sensory cues all around us can trigger all sorts of intense emotions, whether we are aware of it or not.

Despite having had two careers – social work and interior design – that on the surface seem radically different, Emily tells me that she thinks they have much more in common than people think.

'Both are actually about working with people to help them feel happy and safe at home. Social work, particularly working with children, is really all about well-being in the home and supporting people to lead better, happier, healthier lives. And really, it's the same when you're working in interiors.'

Talking to Emily makes me reflect on my own feelings about writing about interiors. When I mention to people that I am writing about homes, I get the feeling that some people are quite surprised. To many, this may seem like a frivolous or shallow topic. There is a pervasive idea that stuff, things, material objects, don't matter. It's an idea that has perhaps been made more popular in recent years by the upsurge in the minimalist movement and in people rejecting consumerism as a reaction to the climate crisis we are facing. The idea that material things don't matter, Emily says, is one that comes from an extremely privileged position.

'Firstly, try telling someone who's got no stuff that stuff doesn't matter! Secondly, an enormous amount of our identity, our self-respect, how much we value ourselves, and how safe and comfortable we feel comes from what we are surrounded by. As humans we naturally tell our stories through our environment and the things we pick and choose to create our homes, but also there is a lot of

evidence that shows the impact that our lived environment has on our physical and emotional well-being.'

I was keen to speak to a beneficiary of Furnishing Futures, so Emily put me in touch with Gemma* , who a year and a half ago was referred to the charity by the domestic violence charity Solace. Gemma had been heavily pregnant when she left her baby's father. Things had become so bad that, when he left the house to go shopping one day, she took her chance to leave, only able to take a bag of clothes with her. Gemma is diabetic and her pregnancy had been extremely difficult. 'I was so unwell,' she tells me, 'the stress of everything with the baby's father, plus health problems during the pregnancy.' With nowhere else to go, Gemma was given temporary accommodation by the council just a week before she was due to be induced early, due to the baby's health. The temporary accommodation had no fridge, no washing machine and no furniture. 'There wasn't even any curtains or blinds and the flat was on a main road,' she tells me. 'I had diabetes medication that needed refrigerating and I was about to go to hospital to have a baby.'

When she was put in touch with Emily, Gemma hoped they might be able to help out with a few essentials. A cot, a bed for herself and a fridge. 'What Emily did was so much more than that. It's impossible to describe, but she thought of absolutely everything.'

While Gemma was being induced, Emily took the keys, measured up the space and got everything Gemma would need to bring her baby home from the hospital. 'Emily asked me questions about what I wanted but honestly, I didn't have any headspace, so I asked if she could make decisions for me.'

Gemma had a difficult labour, followed by an emergency C-section. To ease her worries about going home, Emily took a video of what she had done with the space. 'It really eased my mind. I had been so

*Not her real name.

worried about what would happen when I left the hospital.' But Gemma told me, although she had seen a video, she had been unprepared for what it would be like to walk in. 'Emily had thought of everything I would need, even down to cleaning products, toiletries and nappies for the baby. I would have been grateful for any help, but everything was such high quality and so thoughtful.'

Gemma had been in temporary accommodation once, years before, age 16, when she had been homeless. 'I was there for a year. It was awful. There were rats and cockroaches, and I had no furniture. My mindset at the time was *what's the point?* But after what Emily did, I never once felt like that walking into that accommodation. It was still a really, really difficult time mentally. But because she had made the place homely, it didn't feel impossible.'

Having a stable home to call your own, whether you own it or are a secure social tenant, was once a possibility for most but is increasingly for the lucky and the privileged. My own home was bought eleven years ago when I was still married. It has been mine alone for the past eight and a half years, after my partner and I divorced, and I took on the mortgage alone. This is something that was only possible because my mother died owning her own home, passing it on to me and my brothers, so my mortgage, although still significant, is just about manageable on one income. There isn't a day that goes by that I don't thank my lucky stars that my mother gave me this. Without her, divorce would have meant selling up and losing our home.

When I chat to Gemma, I can hear her 16-month-old baby babbling happily in the background. They have finally moved from the temporary accommodation to a permanent home. It was a huge battle to get here, involving Gemma turning down a number of completely unsuitable homes for a baby, with black mould, collapsing ceilings and evidence of previous leaks and flooding. Gemma works for a housing charity and knew what she was seeing and her right to say no to such places. Many people, made to feel as though they must accept any help, even completely inappropriate properties, aren't as aware of their rights.

Despite Emily making her temporary accommodation work as well as it possibly could, knowing the situation was temporary, and knowing they would be moved out of borough for her and the baby's safety, Gemma could never fully settle. Now they have a permanent and suitable place to live, she can start to think about the future. She has brought everything with her to their new home, but as the temporary accommodation was extremely small, Furnishing Futures are working with her again to help fill those gaps.

Housing insecurity is a problem for increasing numbers of people. The National Housing Federation estimates that 8.5 million people in England are living in unaffordable, insecure and unsuitable homes. It is a crisis that, as Emily points out to me, has a significant effect on health, chronic stress, child development and so much more. In the last twelve months alone, there has been a 5 per cent increase in private rent in the UK and Australia, and around 3.7 million people in the UK are living in overcrowded housing. At the time of writing, forecasters in the US are predicting a 7–8.4 per cent rise in the cost of renting, citing unaffordable mortgages and housing shortages as factors.

'Creating a home, however we can, is an act of self-care and a rebellious one at that.'

In her book *All the Houses I've Ever Lived In*, author and journalist Kieran Yates tells the heart-breaking, raw and occasionally very funny story of the many homes she has lived in and a housing system that is falling apart around us. Raised by a single, immigrant mother, Yates has experienced it all – social housing, private rentals,

sofa surfing in overcrowded houses and student accommodation.
Taking her from notorious run-down London estates, to a Welsh
car showroom and Victorian flats with black mould, her story is a
reflection of the housing crisis that has been on the rise since the
neglect of social housing that began in the 1970s. This was cemented
by Thatcher's Right to Buy scheme, which gave social tenants the
right to buy their council properties at heavily discounted rates,
decimating the social housing stock. Kieran's book is a rallying cry
to change what is changeable – if only the will were there. She
writes that creating a home, however we can, is an act of self-care
and a rebellious one at that.

I think of what having a home of my own means to me as a single
parent, who has a child with very complex needs. He attends a
specialist school. This means, unlike parents of non-disabled
children, I do not have the right to move him to another school if
I feel like it. Educational decisions for disabled children are made
by tribunal. Having secure housing means we can stay in one
spot, which is vital for his emotional well-being as well as access
to his school.

We have grubby paintwork and a long list of repairs and updates that
need attending to. I struggle to keep up with DIY while working and
caring for an autistic child who is prone to tipping over paint cans in
delight, just to watch the colour spread outwards in oozing patterns.
Our ceilings bear the remnants of thrown food, dry rice from sensory
play collects in nooks and crannies, and there is a prominent hole in
the kitchen ceiling from the bathroom being flooded one too many
times by my water-obsessed son. Lights and other fittings are
regularly broken. While these things cause some stress in our lives
and the cost of repairs is a constant background worry for me, one
thing I do not have to worry about is being kicked out. I agree with
Yates that homemaking is an act of self-care. Creating a welcoming
home (and having paid work to pay for it) is an act of self-care for
me as an unpaid carer. I once interviewed a mother who was evicted

from her privately rented flat because the neighbours complained about the repetitive noises her autistic son made. The housing charity Shelter has conducted research that shows you are significantly more likely to face housing discrimination if you are Black, Asian or disabled. Everyone deserves a home they can feel safe in.

*

Northumberland

Even when circumstances are not as challenging as those affecting Furnishing Futures clients, creating a home for ourselves or our family does not always happen in the way we planned or hoped for. This is something I knew I wanted to discuss with author Caro Giles. Her memoir, *Twelve Moons*, tells the story of a year raising her four daughters alone in a small market town at the very top of England. Two of Caro's daughters have complex needs and health issues, and only one out of the four is able to access mainstream schooling. Caro now home-schools out of necessity, writing in the early hours of the morning before her daughters wake. Their home, a Victorian terrace near the sea, is both a safe haven and a compromise.

Caro and I have been friends for a few years, meeting and writing online together since the pandemic began, when we were all trapped in our houses. The two of us bonded over our shared caring responsibilities and our need to carve out time to write. But as the country freed up again, Caro's home remained more closed off than most. Two of her daughters find the world a very difficult place to navigate, so home is where they feel safest and where they want to be most of the time. As a single parent, this means Caro has been largely pinned to the home, too.

My boyfriend, Ruairi, steps in to look after the kids overnight so I can make the long drive up to Northumbria. I travel north for six hours, listening to Barbara Kingsolver's *Demon Copperhead*, watching the bright-yellow rapeseed fields fly by. It feels fitting to be listening to this story now, about a boy shunted from place to place, ignored and abused by systems that should be there to protect him.

'Homes are important to all of us, but for those who find the world to be hostile, who find themselves misunderstood or judged, they are even more important.'

I arrive late, but it is almost midsummer and this far north it is still light. The street is beautiful and exactly how I picture them in northern England. Pretty front gardens, dark stone, handsome solid houses, an alleyway strung with washing lines at the back. The girls have waited up, too excited to go to bed before their visitor arrives. They know my son is autistic, too, and some of them have questions for me about him. Does he speak? Does he like wearing ear defenders? What are his favourite things? I smile and answer their open and curious questions, while eating a late-night bowl of pasta Caro has saved for me. Eventually Caro peels them away to go to bed. We sit and have a cup of tea and she tells me that she thinks they are more relaxed around me because they know I have an autistic child. They are so used to being judged by outsiders, so not all visitors are as welcomed.

Homes are important to all of us, but for those who find the world to be hostile, who find themselves misunderstood or judged, they are even more important. A place to be ourselves when we feel the world wants us to be other than we are.

Caro is keen to stress how lucky she feels to have a safe roof over her head after the end of her marriage, something which so many single parents don't have. But it does feel like a compromise, she tells me. Money is tight while she has no choice but to home-school, and two

of her daughters would not cope at all with a house-move at this stage. Caro has had to reframe her thinking around the idea of home and accept that there are some things that are simply out of her control right now.

I ask her if she has been able to make changes to the physical space in the five years since her ex-husband moved out, and if that has helped. Knowing that moving was not possible, she tells me that reclaiming the home felt important. She had to do it slowly, for the girls' sake, but she tells me it was important to make the space feel palatable to her again. 'It had been drenched in sadness for a really long time,' she says. 'It's a real trauma when your family is cleaved in two, so I needed to find a way to heal and grieve and make it feel like a nice space again.' She began very practically, by just painting a lot of the rooms white and taking any pictures down that made her feel sad.

Next, she created a space for herself to write. She hadn't taken her writing seriously up until that point, so that felt like a really important step. Caro's desk sits on the landing, with a large window beside it looking out over the rooftops. It is not a private room where you can shut the door, but it is a dedicated space that is given over to her writing and creativity. She can sit at it, she tells me, and be surrounded by books, cards and notes from writing friends and readers, and not have to look at piles of laundry or other household things. She can be Caro the writer here. Even though she does also write in other parts of the house, she loves that she has a space just for her work. She thinks it's important for her girls to see her there as well. For them to know that among all her caring responsibilities and all the admin around fighting for her children's needs to be met, she has been able to preserve something for herself, too. She describes the changes she made to the house as 'just as much about trying to find out who I was, and using the space to do that, as well as making the house a nice place to be.'

Chapter Five

As the kids got bigger, Caro moved out of what had been the master bedroom and into the smallest bedroom, to allow the four girls to have the two larger rooms. She struggled and eventually found a double bed that fitted snugly into the room. It touches three sides and sits right under the window. I go to take a look. It's a cosy and peaceful space that feels very Caro. It has fairy lights and candles, to light up the dark northern winter mornings, and a bookshelf that belonged to her granny, and when she lies back in bed at night she can often see the moon right from her pillow. She laughs and says that the bed is so wedged in that it will never come out again. She's happy there now, but she didn't feel great about the move to the smaller bedroom at first.

'It was a big thing at the time,' she says, 'because I didn't know anyone else who did that, who had that situation where the kids had the bigger rooms and there was a single adult in the smallest room. It kind of highlighted my existence as a single parent.'

This is a feeling I am familiar with. There are some aspects of my home that are what they are because of my son's needs, which do sometimes feel like a representation of our differences as a family. A reminder of what sets us apart. Most of the time I embrace our differences, but occasionally, especially when we are having a particularly challenging time, it can sting.

'On the positive side,' Caro tells me, 'sometimes people on the outside look in and they see that this woman has created a space on her landing where she writes and how does she do that? How does she do that with all those children and no time? Yes, she is in the tiny bedroom, but what is she doing there? She's raising her family and writing and she's reading her books and actually lots of people who are in marriages that aren't that happy kind of think it's great that I can be on my own like this.'

She adds: 'For all that this can be hard, I also think it can be brilliant and rebellious and brave. It doesn't always feel like that. Sometimes it's really fucking lonely, but it's still better. Better because it feels true.'

That's how it feels to be in Caro's home. It feels true. A place where her daughters can be themselves without fear of judgement, where they can learn in a way that works for them. It's a place where some of the loveliest details are the smallest, thrown together with what Caro could manage in the circumstances.

'But it felt important to be able to make these choices all on my own.'

I think back to how I reclaimed my home after the end of my marriage. I had no money, so, like Caro, the changes were not big. A reshuffle of some furniture, a reclaimed 1950s kitchen unit given by a friend, new bed linen, the furniture that had belonged to my mother brought out of storage. But it felt important to be able to make these choices all on my own; to allow for the house to evolve and change to fit the life I had now, who I was now, rather than me clinging to the past or some imaginary other life that never happened.

Even though I always worked from home, I didn't have a desk for years. I diligently unpacked and packed up my work things each day. It wasn't until the long lockdowns that I decided it was finally time to give myself a desk. It felt, as Caro put it, rebellious. Being able to continue working as a single parent and unpaid carer has felt like an uphill battle every step of the way. Unlike Caro's girls, my son is able to access a school that meets his needs, but in every other way life can be a fight. With school transport, with social services, with carers who come and go. At every meeting involving the local authority, the

NHS, the school or social services, the expectation is that I can and will drop everything. The idea that I might work, when so many mothers of disabled children cannot (only 3 per cent of mothers of disabled children work full time), draws blank stares of incredulity, as though my need to earn a living to provide for my son makes me a 'difficult' parent. So when I see my desk in the corner of my front room, it does feel rebellious. It feels like a symbol of hope. That I can be on hand for my family, and that I can earn a living and create something, too. That I am more than one thing.

'There is something incredibly powerful about claiming a space as our own, whether it's rented, social housing or owned.'

I know many brilliant and brave single parents. My friend who, after years of moving around our London neighbourhood, where rent is constantly on the increase, moved her kids up to Glasgow to live in a more affordable city and rent a beautiful high-ceilinged flat. Another who said she felt so proud of herself the day she saw the paperwork with only her name on the mortgage. She painted her stairs bright yellow to celebrate. There is something incredibly powerful about claiming a space as our own, whether it's rented, social housing or owned. It's a small piece of control. Even if circumstances mean we cannot create a home exactly as we want or need it to be, we can hopefully build ourselves a desk on the landing and say, 'This, right here, this is mine.'

Chapter Six: Creativity from Constraints

Margate, Kent, and Somerset

There is sometimes a preconception that creating a beautiful and comfortable home is all about how much money you have to spend. As vital as it is to the process of creating a home, money can only take us so far. Some of the most boring, uninspired and uncomfortable homes I have been in have been the wealthiest. Perhaps that is because they are too busy making that money to be able to approach home-making in any other way than to throw cash at it. Or perhaps it is because they place a high importance on social status and their homes reflect that. Whatever the reasons, the fact is that money (beyond a certain point) is not always the answer to the problems of our homes. And finances are far from the only constraints we face. Whether it's being constrained to a certain location because of work or family commitments, a disability or chronic illness that necessitates adaptations or any number of other things beyond our control, the challenges we face in creating our homes are not always fixable with cash. But they don't always have to be the reason our homes are not the beautiful spaces we want them to be either. Sometimes, it's the things that challenge us that create the most interesting homes of all.

Margate, Kent

Emily's instructions for how to get to her home arrive via email with the words 'We are the run-down looking house on the corner' and 'don't be alarmed by the mess'. I laughed when I read it because I had been certain she would tell me there was no way she was ready for me to take pictures of her still-very-much-a-work-in-progress house. But I had asked her anyway, knowing that she was exactly the person I needed to talk to about making do and creative constraints. Luckily for me, embracing imperfection for Emily extended to allowing me to take photos when most other people would have told me to back off. For her, the process and the progress is part of the charm.

Emily Henson is an author, art director and interiors stylist. We first met in 2011 when she returned to London after living for a long time in LA. Since then, she has written and styled five interiors books and styled shoots for some of the country's leading interiors brands. It all began many years ago in LA, when she started blogging about interiors and what goes on behind the scenes of interior styling under the handle Life Unstyled, which eventually became the title of one of her books. Although her job as an art director with brands necessitates working with trends and coming up with highly styled shoots, her work as a writer and editorial stylist is far more about getting creative and using what you already have.

The funny, privileged position you are in as a photographer or stylist is that you are given a glimpse behind the metaphorical curtain, like Dorothy and the Great and Powerful Wizard of Oz, in ways that the average person is not. It is a myth, perhaps unwittingly perpetuated by glossy magazines and now social media, that having plenty of money will solve every issue and compromise a home can come up against. For every person on a budget, no matter how high, there is some choice they could make that would tip it over into unaffordable for them. There will always be bigger houses, more expensive tiles, and higher-end appliances to yearn for, for all but the most obscenely wealthy in our society. And I'm pretty sure they all still complain about not having quite enough. The homeowner who has £5 million to spend on a house is just as likely as the one who has £250,000 to think, *If I just had a little more, it would solve so many problems.*

'Compromise, even the financial kind, can lead to the most beautiful homes imaginable.'

While every single one of us deserves a home that meets our needs and money is a vital aspect of that, it cannot magic away every constraint. And, in fact, the opposite can often be true. Compromise, even the financial kind, can lead to the most beautiful homes imaginable. When forced to make creative decisions when other answers can't easily be found, the compromised home is one that is as unique as a fingerprint and able to meet the homeowners' needs, in a beautiful and imperfect way.

Of course, this does not mean that money is never the answer. The cost of housing in England has changed dramatically over the past few decades. In 1997, 71 per cent of local authorities (LA) in England were considered affordable (meaning the average cost of a home was less than five times the average wage in that same LA). In 2022, that number had fallen to 7 per cent. In the US, house prices have surged by 25 per cent since 2019, accompanied at the same time by a drop in the number of houses available for sale, and in Australia, where the median salary is currently $62,500, the median price of a house is $732,886 (rising to over $1 million in the Sydney area). The cost of renovating has also skyrocketed in recent years, due to the increasing cost of raw materials, so even repairing and maintaining a home is more expensive. I'm not going to pretend that money doesn't matter enormously when it so clearly does. But it's also a case of diminishing returns. After a certain point, more money doesn't get you a better home, it just gets you a more expensive one.

*

Emily's new home that I have come to see is in the seaside town of Margate and is a 1950s bungalow on a quiet street. It is the first home she has owned since she left LA in 2011 and she chose what can only be described as a project. When she and her boyfriend, Lorenzo, put their offer in, they knew they were taking on a lot. The house had barely been touched since it was built, including an original boiler and dangerous electrics, almost no insulation and rotting windows. It's a sweet white house on a corner plot with plenty of garden around it.

Emily shows me in to the kitchen-living room. It's a bright, high-ceilinged space, with a large wooden dining table and a collection of mismatched chairs, a sofa and armchair covered in cushions and throws, and a large kitchen island made from vintage cabinetry from an RAF base. Originally a small kitchen, hallway and living room, Emily tells me that when they bought it she thought she'd simply knock out a doorway between the kitchen and living room and be done with it. But after they got the keys, a friend who is an interior architect walked in and convinced her to knock out the low ceiling so that they could take advantage of the height, and to knock out all the walls, too, allowing the light to come in on all three sides.

Going for this layout was not her first instinct, but she soon realised that for this house it was absolutely the right choice. The ceiling now reaches up into the eaves above the living and dining area, while remaining in place above the kitchen. This has allowed them to create a small loft space upstairs, which will eventually be lit with skylights and turned into a cosy library, with low-level furniture to curl up in with a book. Emily has saved some of the original carpet that they pulled up in the living room, a rich brown and gold floral pattern. 'I cut off a piece big enough for the loft. When it's ready, I'll have [the carpet] cleaned and see if it works up there. I love the idea of reusing it and keeping it here in this home.'

This room seems to sum up Emily's ethos perfectly: making use of the resources you have and giving the space a contemporary twist. The curtains at one of the windows are those that were hanging when they first arrived. They are a rich dark-gold velvet, and when she took them down to wash them, they were still in pretty good condition, so she hung on to them. They would be so expensive to have made, she tells me, so why not reuse them? The IKEA sofa is one she's had for years. 'I cannot imagine spending thousands of pounds on a sofa,' she tells me. 'I really don't think it's about where you buy something from. It's about how much you love it and it's about hanging on to things rather than treating them as disposable.'

'Everything can be used or learned from. And if it can't, it can be lived with until it can be fixed.'

The walls of this side of the house are bare plaster and the floors concrete. Emily and Lorenzo laid the floors themselves. She laughs, saying they got pretty good at it and that the key is doing it fast before it starts to set. She shows me places where there is a patina across the concrete, caused by the sealant they used. 'We made mistakes and learned a lot,' she says with a shrug. She points up to the ceiling above the dining table. There are a lot of pendant light fittings. She tells me that suddenly one day the electrician said she had to make a decision about where she wanted the lights in that room, and she hadn't planned it yet. So he put in too many. 'There are some things I would do differently.' She tells me that as a stylist she can make a lot of decisions on the fly but perhaps hadn't quite realised just how many needed to be planned for in a renovation of this scale. But the thing I love about Emily's attitude is that she doesn't fuss over the mistakes. Everything can be used or learned from. And if it can't, it can be lived with until it can be fixed.

So often, I have met homeowners who have tried to do absolutely everything at once and get everything right first time. But this is not how homes work. Even the most experienced interiors expert gets things wrong and knows the benefit of taking things slowly. A lot of the beauty comes from the mistakes and the unplanned detours. And some of the beauty comes from the compromises and the making do, too.

We sit down at Emily's dining table with coffee and talk about what brought her here. As someone who has made a living styling interiors, she did not mean to be a renter for so long. Emily is British and she spent her teenage years in nearby Broadstairs but upped and moved to New York aged seventeen. Her children were born in LA and their dad is American, too, so when they left LA for London in 2011 they didn't sell their house there, not knowing how it would pan out. On a whim and a recommendation from Emily's cousin, they rented a house in Stoke Newington. The kids settled into school and Emily into her life as an interior stylist and writer in London. By the time they knew they wanted to stay, they realised they had settled into an area too expensive for them to buy a home in. She tells me that the home they were renting was literally falling apart and needed to be completely gutted, and yet when the owners put it on the market it sold for well over a million pounds. 'It was so depressing,' she says.

When Emily and her then husband separated, with her kids in secondary school and having already moved across the world once, she was loath to leave the area and make them start over. So she rented a modern flat near the kids' school. 'I really hated it at first,' she tells me. 'It didn't feel like me at all.' But the location was great and it turned into an easy place to live in those years post-separation. During the lockdowns in 2020, her eldest, now at university, returned home. Emily, like all of us working in interiors photography, lost all of her work. She was paying a fortune to live in a flat she didn't love. Her son was doing his A levels and she realised during that time that very shortly she would be freed up from being in that area. The house in LA now sold, if she wanted to stay in London, she tells me, she could have probably afforded something very tiny. But for the first time, she realised, she was yearning to leave, come to the sea and have a little more space. Her own space.

In 2021 she left her London flat and rented a small Victorian flat on the Kent coast, near to where she had grown up, so she could begin her search. She bid on several other homes, but they all fell through. Eventually, she and Lorenzo found this bungalow. This is not the home she had been expecting to buy. She had imagined herself living in a tall Victorian house with lots of cosy rooms. 'I'm so glad none of those earlier ones worked out,' she tells me. The bungalow may have been more of a beast to take on than they had first realised, but

Emily now can't imagine living anywhere else. This quirky 1950s home has completely stolen her heart.

She and Lorenzo are doing as much of the work themselves as they can and bringing in tradespeople and builders as needed. Her current project, when I visit, is her home studio where she has decided to keep the original lino tiles and is experimenting with different clear coatings, to polish them up a bit. The curtains are original, a sweet cottage-style floral print, but she tells me they'll probably go. 'I like them, but they might be a bit too twee, too retro,' she says. As much as Emily loves vintage pieces, she also likes it to feel fresh and contemporary. The yellow tiled bathroom is about to get ripped out and the layout redesigned. She has just been waiting for a long enough stretch between shoots to tackle the job. The plan is for the builder to return to put skylights in the reading loft and, eventually, they'll have to replace more windows and get some insulation into the bedroom side of the house, which currently has none. There is a lot to do, but rather than being overwhelmed by it, Emily tells me she's trying to embrace and enjoy the process. 'This is what I wanted after years of renting and not being allowed to do anything.'

Emily's latest book, *Create*, is all about creativity over consumption. She firmly believes that we should be making do, reusing what we have and using our creativity to create our homes, not just because it's more sustainable, but because of the satisfaction and joy of creating something original. Emily admits that, like me, she can be uncomfortable sometimes with the commercial side of her job. We are both hired to make brands look very desirable, which in turn encourages consumption. So she decided long ago that her editorial work would counter that and be far more in line with her own personal philosophy. Her book *Life Unstyled* is all about embracing imperfection and encouraging people to accept that life is in constant flux, and your home will change and evolve as you do. It is one of my favourite interiors books, filled with creative, cluttered homes

and unusual spaces that owners have made work for them. This is not how most interiors are presented.

'I was recce-ing homes for a big brand shoot last year,' she says. 'I think I visited thirteen in two days, and after a few I realised they were all exactly the same. All Victorian, with a dark-painted living room, a massive extension with identical Crittall glass doors. Quite maximalist, with bold colours. But they were all exactly the same.' A lot of money will give you a house that has a certain kind of status. But is it necessary to create a home? Emily and I have seen the inside of a lot of houses of all kinds over the years and we both agree: a lot of money does not make a house a home.

Not everyone is willing or able to lay their own concrete floor or try their hand at many of the jobs Emily is getting stuck into in her home, and nor does she expect everyone to. But through her work as a writer, she's encouraging people to think about approaching their homes in a way that embraces imperfection.

The 1950s bungalow is a slow renovation. It's been about eighteen months now and there are many years to go. 'I don't have young kids at home anymore, which I totally see gives me the opportunity to do this slower and live with more mess than many people can,' she says. But having an attitude that allows things to evolve slowly frees you up in a different way. She laughs at the idea of being 'done' with this home and tosses around the idea of extending up into the loft one day or adding a side extension. There are so many possibilities and it's exciting, but she doesn't feel the need to do all of it now. Right now, she and Lorenzo are doing what they can with the budget they have. They could stretch themselves, spend more, borrow more. But she wants to take her time, allow the house to change over time and them to feel more secure financially. It is not worth getting themselves into a difficult financial position just to go fast and more expensive.

As I move around the house and take photos, Emily styles and shifts things about. I think of all the times a homeowner has apologised to me for some rooms in the house not being quite finished, or tidy enough, many of them under the impression that I expect perfection. But even editorial shoots are a kind of fiction. A story told. Not dishonest or made up, but in choosing where to direct the viewer's gaze, a lot is left out.

Despite its partially completed state, Emily is excited I'm here. It's the first time anyone has photographed her house and she enjoys seeing it on screen in its current form. 'It will be a record of how it was on this day. By the time the book is published, it will probably look very different. I love that,' she says.

Spending time in Emily's slow renovation has reminded me of the beauty of making do and taking things one step at a time instead of thinking that money holds all the answers, but I also want to look at a different kind of constraint – one that many people are faced with.

*

Somerset

I pull up into a long, tree-lined driveway. The heavy grey clouds of the morning have lifted, leaving blue skies, warmth and a breeze. I have finally made it to Somerset and my friend Alex comes out to greet me. It's been over eighteen months since I was last here, a recurrent theme among my old friends. Between kids, school, work schedules and not living nearby to each other anymore, this phase of our lives makes it particularly hard to hang out.

Alex and I became friends in our mid-twenties; I was a fashion photographer's assistant, he a stylist's assistant. We spent many weeks (probably months) on trips to deserts, glaciers, mountains, beaches and country estates, shooting from dawn until dusk, keeping each other company on long plane and car rides and in the most magnificent locations. When I was offered my first book shoot, I gave part of my meagre budget to Alex to style it, and it was the project that helped us both leave assisting behind forever.

The farmhouse Alex and his wife, Anneke, have lived in for the past seven years, Bridle Farm, dates back to the 1600s. Unusually, the footprint of the vast majority of the house is original, the Georgian additions that came later being only a brick facade, rather than cobbled-together extra rooms or wings. This, it turns out, is quite crucial to the reason they chose the farmhouse in the first place, because it meant there were a few features they could take advantage of.

Bridle Farm's ground floor, unusually for such an old house, is all on one level. There are no steps, high thresholds or strange additional rooms, and most of the outside areas around it are flat, too. The original doorways are all extra-wide, having been built to allow room for livestock. This makes it a house able to adapt much better to a wheelchair than most old Grade II listed houses. Anneke was diagnosed with multiple sclerosis (MS) in her late twenties. When they bought the house she was already using a cane regularly. She now uses an electric wheelchair all the time.

Alex and Anneke always knew that they would live in the country. 'We grew up as muddy kids, and we knew we wanted our kids to be muddy, too,' she tells me with a laugh over lunch. I think back to the first time Alex introduced me to Anneke. We

were at a music festival in Wales and Anneke arrived with a proper
yurt, which she constructed and laid out with beds and sheepskins,
rugs and even a wood-burning stove. Over the tea she made for me
on that stove, she told me how much she hated London, where Alex
was living at the time, and that he would never be able to drag her
there. I remember laughing and thinking Alex had definitely met his
match. I never saw Alex as a London kind of person either. He made
more sense in the country, in a pair of wellies and a thick wool coat.

They moved to southwest Wales, where Alex had grown up, and
rebuilt a Victorian farmhouse on a steep Welsh hillside. Alex did a lot
of the work himself in between travelling for shoots. Anneke, a
landscape gardener, built the walled kitchen garden. It was a
beautiful, very remote spot and it became clear to Anneke that it was
not going to work long term. She had already been diagnosed with
MS and her future health and mobility were uncertain. They decided
to move to Bath, where their son Freddie was born. After a few years,
they were yearning for the countryside and sold their house. They
thought they would have to rent for a while, thinking their wish list of
needs was too long to find anything quickly. But almost immediately
Anneke found the listing for Bridle Farm, and when they saw it she
knew instantly that it was home. There was potential for accessibility
and the house was uncannily like Anneke's childhood home.

Anneke had grown up in rural Wiltshire in a thatched millhouse
with a river running right beside it. She knew she was looking for
that same feeling of home and she found it at Bridle Farm. The first
time I saw it, almost seven years ago, I was stopping by on my way
to a shoot in Cornwall. They had moved straight in, despite the fact
that it was very run down. The previous elderly owner, as happens so
often, had retreated to one single room and the rest of the house had
been left unused for years. We sat around the wood-burning stove in
the old kitchen and Anneke had beamed and declared that she
wouldn't leave this house unless it was in a wooden box.

A lot has changed since I was here last. Eighteen months ago, Anneke was using a mobility scooter outside of the house but was on her feet inside, relying on walking sticks and a walking frame when she needed it. She's now permanently using an electric wheelchair, after a series of falls made it clear the time had come. As we sit down to lunch on the back patio, I ask her how the adaptations to the house are holding up since the move to using a wheelchair inside. 'Terrible!' she says with a dark laugh. 'We thought we had really thought things through but there is so much we didn't consider.'

As you approach the house, it's now via a long, smooth concrete drive – a recent addition that Alex tells me is the most boring and best money he has ever spent. It allows their children to chase each other on bikes in large circles and gives Anneke the freedom to get in and out of their WAV (wheelchair-accessible vehicle) van without then trekking muddy tire tracks through the house. The door to the large kitchen-diner is original and double width, leading straight onto the original flagstone floors. This large room had originally been a number of smaller ones, but now it's open, with exposed beams and the addition of some front and side glazed dormers to flood it with light. The room is wide enough so that Anneke can manoeuvre pretty well around the dining table, and all around the kitchen. The kitchen, however, was planned around Anneke's previous mobility needs. Although they had made sure to allow room for a wheelchair to access the whole ground floor, the kitchen itself was designed for standing height.

Alex had two sinks put in, so that there was one directly next to the AGA where the kettle sits. Anneke had only to move the long neck of the pot filler tap to the right to be able to fill the kettle up where it sat on the stove, so she didn't have to walk across the room carrying the kettle. It also meant she could drain pasta directly into the sink from the stove in one movement. The large kitchen island was placed so that Anneke was always within reach of a surface if she needed it, never having to lift and carry anything too far. 'It worked well for a while,' Alex says.

'Disability is not a fixed thing, with
many people experiencing chronic
illnesses that change significantly
over time and progressive conditions
that mean their needs change at an
unpredictable rate.'

I ask whether they will lower one of the sinks or surfaces now, and
Anneke shakes her head. It's hard to know what's worth it, she tells
me. She has lost almost all the use of her right arm, and her left is
quite weak, too. This is one of the most difficult aspects of Anneke's
disability. The constant uncertainty it brings means that making
decisions about anything, including adaptations to the house, is
frustratingly hard. Contrary to what many believe, a lot of disabled
people have this experience. Disability is not a fixed thing, with many
people experiencing chronic illnesses that change significantly over
time and progressive conditions that mean their needs change at an
unpredictable rate.

'It's also a chicken-and-egg situation,' Anneke tells me. 'When I
moved to using this chair after a couple of falls, although it's much
safer for me, I didn't quite realise how much muscle tone I would
lose just by not taking those few steps here and there.' So although
she's grateful that the chair keeps her safe and helps her get around,
she's very aware that she's lost even more muscle since she started
using it full time.

The family bedrooms are upstairs, but one of the aspects of the
house that is very practical is it has an old bakehouse attached to
the kitchen. The first thing Alex did was adapt this into a bedroom
with an accessible bathroom. It's a high-ceilinged room with a
wood-burning stove in the original, large chimney and windows
overlooking the back garden. The plan was to use it as a room for an

au pair or a carer if they needed it while Alex travelled for work, and then, in time, for Anneke to use when the stairs became impractical. She has been using it for some time now and they have been making small changes to make it work as well as possible, such as the recently added thick, cosy carpet over the top of the stone floors, and a sleeping mezzanine, which Alex added for the kids so that they could sleep closer to their mum at night when they want to. Anneke tells me that despite the fact that they thought ahead about this, they still didn't quite get it right. They recently had to remove the bathroom door entirely because it was just too challenging for her to manage later in the day when she was exhausted. 'I should have asked for more advice from other disabled people and accessibility companies when we were building,' she says. 'Hindsight is a beautiful thing.'

But then again, they couldn't prepare for every single eventuality either, not knowing exactly how and when Anneke's needs would change. Without knowing exactly what the future holds, and with all these adaptations proving hugely expensive, particularly in a Grade II listed house, it's not easy to know what to fight for or what is more important to pay for.

We sit around the outdoor table, eating Alex's homemade Eton mess. When the kids are done they abandon us for their bikes and race off down the drive. 'Tell me about the best things you did here,' I say to them both, when the kids are out of sight. Without even taking a moment to think about it, Anneke points to the paving-stone ramp, which goes from the patio area, where we are sitting, to the rest of the garden, where there is a kitchen garden, a small orchard and a view of the fields beyond.

'That is the absolute best thing we did.' Even before Anneke needed to use a wheelchair all the time, they knew it was important to keep everything as flat as possible to minimise falls and make it easy for her to get around. They had to lower the patio about half a foot from where it was originally to make it completely flat for access to the house, and then there was a step up to the rest of the garden, so the ramp was constructed of the same stone as the patio. 'When your world becomes very small, these things are really important,' she tells me.

Although my disabled son requires a lot of support, he doesn't have the kinds of mobility needs that most people think of when they think about accessibility. But like Anneke's, our world can be small for different reasons, and we have had to make other kinds of adaptations to keep him safe. All the upstairs windows have additional locks that prevent them opening more than about a hand's width. This is not because he might fall or jump out, but because he went through a very long phase of enjoying watching things fly out of the window. We went through a lot of toilet paper before I had those locks installed. He loved to watch them fly like streamers out of the bathroom window. And I still occasionally find an old bath toy or toothbrush when I'm digging in the garden.

We have no mirrors in the house at all, except for the one inside the door of my wardrobe. He has broken too many of them. Curtains and blinds have to be regularly replaced because they are torn and broken. I have lost countless mugs and glassware during meltdowns and replaced every light fitting in the house at least once (some many more times than that). I have swept up more broken lightbulbs than I care to think about.

None of these are a particularly big deal, compared to needing a home to be wheelchair accessible. But always in my mind are the questions, *Is that safe?* and, *Will I be able to afford to replace that?* It is hard to explain the heart-stopping feeling of seeing your child smash a full-length mirror and delightedly start picking up and playing with the shards, unaware of the extreme danger of what they are doing. Better to give up mirrors than to deal with that too often.

Occasionally I wonder how it must feel to make decisions in a house based only on what I would like and what I could afford and not what meets my son's needs. Sometimes in houses I'm shooting, I imagine the kinds of choices I might make if I wasn't constantly thinking about danger, replacing and repairing. But like all aspects of life that we cannot control, it's a futile experiment. The fact is, our house has to meet all of our needs equally. This is my son's home and his world is small. He deserves for this home to be as accessible and free for him to move about in as possible. No beautiful and impractical object, furnishing or layout is worth giving that up for.

I rebel in small ways, though. Many people have suggested over the years that I simply have no breakable objects in the house at all. Learn to drink from plastic cups and eat off plastic plates. Take down all art. Keep everything behind locked doors. But that is not for me either. So I have learned to accept that favourite mugs get smashed, and I have had a lot of practice in the art of letting go.

Still around the table with Alex and Anneke, lunch now finished, I think back to the first time I met Anneke in that yurt in a wet and muddy field in Wales, and although I think I know the answer to my next question, I ask it anyway. 'Do you regret leaving the city? Has it been worth it?'

Anneke looks around at the back of the house, which still has its original stone and mullioned windows, and shakes her head. 'I knew this was home as soon as I saw it.' Neither of them could believe they had found a house that might be able to meet some of Anneke's needs. The wide doors, the completely flat ground floor, the bakehouse. I can't think of many people who would be brave enough to take on a Grade II listed house when they knew many adaptations would have to happen over time. But Alex and Anneke have never been the kind of couple to compromise on what's most important to them. Anneke wanted her kids to have a childhood like her own and Alex's. Bridle Farm has given them exactly that, even

if it's been hugely challenging. The adaptations they have made are imperfect and there is much that they could have done differently if they'd had a crystal ball. But they have never regretted this house.

I follow Anneke up the ramp and around the back of the house to the kitchen garden, which has pumpkins, sweet peas and giant marrows growing in it. In the orchard we find the kids climbing an apple tree and pelting the fallen apples at each other, laughing with glee. It is completely magical here and I can see exactly why Alex and Anneke have come up with every creative adaptation imaginable to make this happen for them. Anneke's health has been very precarious this year and it has made them both reflective. The future holds enormous uncertainty. But one thing they are certain of is that the smaller Anneke's world gets, the more important Bridle Farm becomes, even with all its compromises and imperfections.

Chapter Seven:
The Joyful Home
Stanmore, Greater London, and Usk, Wales

We might need our homes to function well and be practical, but our needs as humans go beyond the basic necessities that make our lives run smoothly. When we think of home and not simply housing, we might think of safety, warmth, comfort, connection and family. For me, all of those things are linked in some way to the pleasure we take from our homes. How can our homes sustain us and help us lead the lives we want to lead? They can do that when we go beyond the practical and remember to lean in to joy.

'We can access tiny moments of joy all around us, by noticing and observing it and by crafting it.'

Ingrid Fetell Lee has written extensively about the aesthetics of joy. What I love most about her work is her belief that joy is not something you just find, it's something you create. We can access tiny moments of joy all around us, by noticing and observing it and by crafting it. This kind of joy is not about exotic holidays and expensive experiences or purchases. It's about taking the time to observe small things that, when added up, can make a huge difference to our lived experience. In her book *Joyful: The Surprising Power of Ordinary Things to Create Extraordinary Happiness*, Ingrid writes about how dismissive we can be about the happiness that can be gained by seeking out joyful aesthetics. She gives the example of someone confessing to her that fresh flowers make her incredibly happy, but she thought it was too extravagant to buy them every week. This same person spent as much in a single therapy session as it would cost to buy themselves flowers every week for a year.

Just as behavioural designer Karen Haller spoke about with me (see page 92), Ingrid, who is a former design director of design consultancy IDEO in New York, writes that aesthetics speak to us on an unconscious level. Perhaps that's why it's so easy for us dismiss them as unimportant. How many times have we heard phrases like 'what it looks like is unimportant, it's what's inside that counts'? In a time of financial hardship for so many, it can be so easy to dismiss aesthetics as frivolous and a distraction from what's important. But what if we can boost our overall happiness by leaning in to joy in our homes?

This is a topic that has deeply interested me since having a disabled child. There are a lot of experiences that he is cut off from, that are inaccessible to him and to us as a family. But my son has never had a problem finding and creating joy. He experiences aesthetics in an intense way due to his sensory challenges. He seems much more tapped in to how aesthetics make him feel and is constantly seeking out stimulation that makes him happy as well as calm. I have learned a lot about how much pleasure we can get from simply paying attention to the aesthetics around us and creating lots of opportunities in our day for tiny moments of joy.

Stanmore, Greater London

On a quiet lane off an ancient-looking village green, I find the house I'm looking for. It's a beautiful red-brick cottage that was formerly two. It is peak wisteria season, and the house is covered in green and purple. It's like something out of a picture book. It wouldn't be that unusual, given that I'm in England, except for the fact that I'm in the north-western London suburb of Stanmore and this is not exactly what I was expecting as I drove through twentieth-century suburban streets to get here. Kemi Lawson greets me at the door. I immediately smile as I look around and know that I have come to exactly the right place to have a conversation about joyful interiors. The entrance is low-ceilinged and not particularly large, but there is so much to grab my eye, I don't know quite where to look first. The wallpaper has repeating illustrations of grand Haitian houses, complete with tropical trees and even a young woman reading. Layered over the wallpaper are artworks and personal photos, and the steep old steps that climb up to the first floor are in a striped, green fabric. A small

glazed internal window gives me a glimpse through into the living room.

Kemi is the founder of The Cornrow, an online interiors boutique, specialising in homeware, books and lifestyle products that celebrate the Black experience. Kemi, who previously worked in finance, decided to launch the business with her sister Lara, after spending time doing up her home and realising there were so few businesses out there whose focus is a modern Black aesthetic.

She takes me into her living room to sit and chat. The room is wallpapered in a gorgeous green, with texture woven into it, giving it an incredible warmth. The sofa and chairs are a mix of different geometric fabrics, and the cushions are made from a variety of fabrics featuring Black women. It feels both luxurious and playful at the same time.

Kemi was born in London to a Jamaican mother and Nigerian father. They moved to Nigeria when she was six, spending holidays in Jamaica with her maternal grandmother, and she returned to England at thirteen to go to boarding school. She describes her taste as a convergence of all those influences: the grand houses of Lagos and Kingston and the Caribbean front-room aesthetic of her maternal grandmother, mixed with a little of the English country-house style of her school.

Kemi tells me that sourcing everything she wanted for the house was really challenging. She was increasingly frustrated that there were no magazines or books or stores that showed the kind of Afro-aristo aesthetic she was interested in. 'It was so difficult to find anything that wasn't portraying Africa and Black culture through a rural, colonial gaze,' she tells me.

'I love stories, I love history and learning about my ancestors, and I think I have poured all of that into my home. I love that my house has motifs that go back generations.'

Kemi's daughters are nine and eleven and were a big part of why she wanted the house to feel so joyful and playful.

'As a Black woman,' she says, 'outside the home is not always joyful.' Micro-aggressions and feeling overlooked in the workplace is a common experience when you are living as a minority in a society, she tells me, so it felt extra important to her that her girls had a safe and happy place to call home. 'I was looking for motifs, colours and art that celebrated us as Black people and celebrated our culture.'

Kemi shows me around the room. She tells me that everything in her home, whether conscious or unconscious, connects her to her past. 'Interiors are the place where everything converges,' she tells me. The fabric on the sofa is a geometric pattern reminiscent of traditional African mathematical designs, as are the tiles in one of the fireplaces. The beanbag is made up of adire fabric that is traditionally used for dressmaking. On the wall is a hand-stitched Asafo flag from Ghana and throughout the room are African Modernist vases and collected objects, which, aside from being beautiful, connect Kemi to things that interest her deeply.

'I love stories, I love history and learning about my ancestors, and I think I have poured all of that into my home. I love that my house has motifs that go back generations.'

She also wanted guests to experience the playfulness and magic when they visit. She takes me back out to the hall, where tucked beside the stairs is a wall, papered with an image of old library bookshelves. There is a light switch on it, which she pushes aside to reveal a keyhole, and then she opens the door. Inside, to my surprise, is her husband's home office.

The house feels much bigger than the exterior suggests. It has hidden nooks everywhere and I imagine what an incredible hide-and-seek house it must make. Because it was once two cottages, there are two staircases, which means the house is connected in a circle. You don't have to go back down the way you came. The long, window-lined hallway upstairs is painted a rich ochre yellow and the stairway is wallpapered with Haitian design house Yaël & Valérie's Past and Connections series, which features repeating illustrations of six Black women through history. Kemi tells me she loves the idea that her girls, whose bedrooms are just off the top of the stairs, see these powerful Black women every time they come downstairs in the morning. 'And the ochre is such a joyful colour, too,' she adds with a smile.

She leads me down the yellow hall to the family bathroom. 'My husband and the girls asked me to do one plain room,' she says with a laugh. 'I agreed, but I said that I just wanted to add a few special tiles.' She opens the door onto a smart grey bathroom. Above the bath there is a splash of colour: six handmade tiles designed by Balineum, which feature the profiles of Black women with different hairstyles. The background colours range from a rich dark brown, through to red, blue, then yellow, representing the earth, the sky and the sun. As with so many other aspects of Kemi's home, I can't help but smile at this. Without the tiles, it would be a very nice bathroom, but it could have belonged to anyone, or even a hotel. These six small tiles totally transform the room.

Kemi shows me into her bedroom and it's like walking into a cloud. The wallpaper, which wraps around the entire room, is a painterly cloudy sky, which darkens slightly towards the ceiling. The light fitting hovers like a fluffy cloud above the bed, which has a throw across it decorated with the phrase 'The blacker the berry, the sweeter the juice' and artwork by illustrator Octavia Mingerink. It's a completely enchanting room, one that I dreamed of when I was eleven – I begged my parents to paint my bedroom blue and hang white curtains at the window so that I could pretend I was sleeping up in the sky. It is somehow bold and serene all at the same time.

'A home should be as personal to you as a fingerprint.'

I ask Kemi about whether she thinks it takes confidence to decorate a home like this and she agrees that it does. She ascribes part of her confidence to the maximalist style of her grandmother's Caribbean front room, a style that is now immortalised in the Museum of the Home in East London, which gives us an idea of how influential this particular aesthetic has been on British interiors.

'A home should be as personal to you as a fingerprint,' Kemi says. When she goes into someone else's home, she wants to know about them, their personality, their history, not something generic. And she agrees, maybe that takes confidence, but adds, 'What's the worst that could happen? You can repaint, you can change wallpaper. It's not that big a deal.'

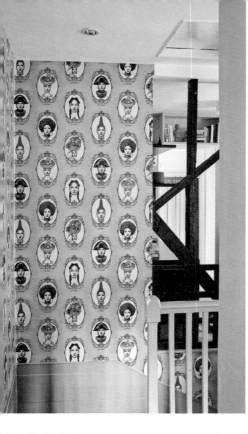

Walking around this home, it's impossible to separate the house from Kemi herself. Her history is woven into the very fabric of it, and I can see the passion behind The Cornrow.

In the beginning, she tells me, The Cornrow was launched to address the problem of representation. When she and Lara made the decision to go ahead, it was around the time of George Floyd's murder in 2020 and suddenly there was a reckoning happening in the media of just how bad underrepresentation was. 'I would read all these interiors magazines and there would not be one Black person, or person of colour, so it's easy to think, Oh, no one's doing it. But people are doing it; we wanted to help people find these businesses.'

'It was important at first to see representation,' she says. She has an original piece of art that is of a girl with an Afro playing the violin. It might sound simple, she explains, but you don't often see Black girls featured in that kind of artwork, and she wanted her own daughters to be able to see that. She tells me about getting an email from a white Irish man with a Black granddaughter, thanking her for the jewellery box with a Black ballerina (instead of the more typically available white ballerina) and how much it meant to him that he could get that for her. The Cornrow sells many gorgeous cushions, original artworks and prints that feature Black people, including their bestselling Black mermaid cushion.

Although physical representation was Kemi and Lara's driving motivation to begin with, The Cornrow has grown to represent much more than that. They are able to promote and make accessible African and Black British artists and designers of all kinds, now including abstract art and design, too. It is a celebration of modern Black aesthetics in every sense. Kemi can promote and spread the Black joy that she so wanted to have reflected in her own home to the many others who want that, too. Her home is a reflection of all these values and pleasures coming together – her ancestry, her history and the pleasure-filled aesthetic of West Africa and Caribbean homes, all woven into the bones of a nineteenth-century English cottage.

*

When I think of joy in my own home, my mind immediately goes to the items that have no practical use whatsoever, but which bring me huge amounts of pleasure. Art. There is no reason at all why I should have a wall hanging above the sofa or a watercolour in my bedroom. No reason except that they are beautiful, they remind me of people I love, they make me pause and even give me a boost without me being conscious of it.

If I think about all the things I have spent money on in this house, I can hands down say that aside from buying the house itself, the most precious item I've paid for with my own cash is a small watercolour painting by the British artist Chloë Cheese. I remember the day I bought it. It was February and there had been a snowstorm. I was living in Borough in London and I walked through the snow to the South Bank where there was an exhibition at the Bankside Gallery by St Jude's, an online gallery showcasing British printmakers. I'd had it marked in my diary for weeks. I made my way around the gallery, thinking that I would allow myself to purchase a print. But then I saw the watercolour and I completely fell in love with it. It features a pear and a mug, sitting on a Poole Pottery plate. It is pretty and whimsical and everything I love about still lifes. I spent the equivalent of half a mortgage payment on that piece, wondering all the while if I had lost my mind. But I didn't have kids yet and work was going well. It felt reckless and extravagant, and perhaps that was part of the desire to own it. I wondered if I would regret spending the money on it.

In the past fifteen years since I bought that painting, I have regretted many purchases. Clothes that didn't fit right, cheap furniture that didn't last, expensive light fittings that were not worth the spend. But I have never, for a single moment, regretted buying that painting.

I don't own a huge amount of original artwork. I had children soon
after the purchase of the Chloë Cheese and it has been hard to justify
it since. I own a very small original painting by Charlotte Keates,
purchased not long after my divorce. Again, buying art as a single
parent felt completely rebellious and I love seeing it beside my bed
each morning. But otherwise, I have mostly limited-edition prints, the
wall hanging and a lot of postcards. They all bring me an enormous
amount of pleasure.

I decided to ask arts journalist and novelist Chloë Ashby about the
desire to have art in our homes. As a journalist, Chloë writes about
and reviews art with a capital A – the kind of art that is owned by
national institutions or multimillionaires. In her first novel, *Wet
Paint*, her protagonist is obsessed with a painting by Manet in the
Courtauld Institute and visits it daily in the aftermath of the
traumatic death of a close friend. She tells me that the art in her
home is deeply cherished, such as pieces by her step-uncle that she
has collected over the years, or things she has from artists she has
interviewed, and a linocut she bought for her husband for their first
anniversary. 'Every artwork in my house reminds me of a place,
person or moment,' she says.

'Art in itself is not necessary for
survival in the same way that the
shelter our homes provide is.
But it can connect us to emotions,
to our pasts and to others in ways
that can hugely enhance our lives.'

But Chloë is also a huge fan of the humble postcard. She tells me she
can't leave an exhibition without buying two or three. Some end up
being used as thank-you notes and birthday cards, and she tells me

that it feels like a nice way of sharing the pleasure she took in seeing the art in real life. Others end up on her pinboard beside her desk, which changes depending on what she's working on. Her very own exhibition space.

'I think, for me, it's partly about inspiration – art has always inspired me, and so surrounding myself with it feels like a safety net. And I also think it's about comfort, and a sense of gathering together artworks and artists in the same way I would gather together friends.'

Humans have always created art. Why? Art can convey beauty and emotion; it can be used to communicate, tell stories, recall memories and emotions, and to educate. While some of those things are functional, art in itself is not necessary for survival in the same way that the shelter our homes provide is. The value it can bring is less tangible. But it can connect us to emotions, to our pasts and to others in ways that can hugely enhance our lives.

I decide to try to find out more about the benefits of owning and displaying art, and I find the perfect person to talk to about it.

*

Usk, Wales

I get up very early one morning and hop in my car, not stopping until I'm over the Welsh border. I have come to see Sonia Pang, curator and owner of Gallery At Home. A former university lecturer in fine art photography, Sonia turned to curating when illness meant she had to take a step back from her work as a lecturer. With her health poor, but itching to get stuck into some work, she set up an exhibition in her own home and it was a roaring success.

I make my way up the drive across a paddock and arrive at the front of the beautiful Welsh longhouse. Sonia and her partner and her youngest child moved in late last year and they are still working on

the house. She greets me at the door, and we sit down in the dark, simply furnished living room to have a coffee and a chat.

'Gallery spaces can be so reverent,' she tells me. Part of what she is trying to achieve with Gallery At Home – which is actually in a gallery space now and no longer based in her home – is a way for people to connect with art accessibly. To show how art can work in a home setting. Art is for everyone, and it doesn't always feel that way when it's viewed in a gallery.

'I curate my home,' she says. 'It's completely intrinsic to my mental health. I do it on a multi-sensory level. I use art, furniture, music, fragrance. It brings me a huge amount of joy.' In the room we are sitting in, there is a wall-length shelf running across it, which currently houses a large piece of work by one of her artists, Toril Brancher – a photographic print on aluminium of a large head of cow parsley. Along the shelf is a single stem in a bud vase, a candlestick and some other small objects. I ask her if she changes the display around much and she laughs.

'It was different this morning and it will be different again tomorrow.' This is the whole point of the long shelf. It allows her to move her displays around with ease, whenever she gets the itch to do so. Sonia doesn't just see the kind of work she sells in her own gallery as art. She brings nature from the outdoors in, puts together collections of objects, including ceramics and glass as well as found objects. She displays some of her own work, too. There is a small print of two girls in white Victorian nightgowns – her daughters, now both grown up, when they were young. It was taken with a pinhole camera. It is a piece of art on its own as well as being wrapped in memories for Sonia of the day she took it, of the choice of the nightgowns and the experiments with the homemade camera. Layers of visual cues all in one small white rectangle. It is more than just a photograph.

'The shelf, for me, is allowing something to be temporary, fluid and changeable. It can be fresh and seasonal. It can house objects, ceramics, photographs, paintings. Anything. It's all artwork. Their value is dictated by the gaze of the viewer.'

Upstairs in her calm and sparsely furnished bedroom, Sonia shows me a display on her chest of drawers. It has personal objects on it that are deeply meaningful to her, many of them given to her by her daughters. When does a simple object become art? It's all about context, value and display, she tells me. When very personal objects are curated and brought together in a way that takes their visual elements as well as their meaning into account, they become art. 'I've curated things so that they are visually appealing to anyone, but for me they have layers of meaning and memory, too. To me, they are emotive. They keep me connected to my family, to people I love.'

When it comes to the art we buy, Sonia tells me, one of the problems is that we start worrying about things like value. Are we making a good investment? She doesn't think that's the question you need to be asking yourself when it comes to art.

She tells me the story of when she was married to her first husband and her daughters were very young. They had just bought a house and they had no money, but they had the opportunity to buy an Ernest Zobole painting, which was £495. They raided their overdraft to buy it and brought it back to their new home. They didn't even own a bed at the time. She said maybe that was crazy, not to buy a bed but to buy a painting instead. Zobole has since died and the painting, which is upstairs in Sonia's office, is now worth about £5,000. 'Would I ever sell it? No way! I remember the night we bought it. I remember the joy of hanging it in our home. The value is in the painting itself and the memories, not the monetary value. That painting is thirty years old and I still look at it and get joy from it.' So what does it matter that it was technically a 'good investment' if Sonia has no intention of selling it? It doesn't matter at all.

'Art is essential. It's as fundamental as music and food and all the other cultural things we seek out to make life richer. What's the point otherwise?' she says.

I find this an interesting thing to point out. There are lots of things we do as humans that might be deemed unnecessary for survival. We could eat very basic, well-balanced diets with no fuss or frills or flavour if we were only eating to survive. We could communicate everything through facts rather than fiction. We could speak instead of sing. We could live in warm and dry but completely unadorned homes. But we don't.

'Art is as fundamental as music and food and all the other cultural things we seek out to make life richer. What's the point otherwise?'

'The artwork we have in our homes, it's the colour we bring into our lives. Otherwise, we're just living in a box. Even if we were stuck in a cell, we'd probably scratch some markings onto the wall.'

Sonia tells me about the book *The Thoughtful Dresser* by Linda Grant, in which she explores why clothing and adornments are so important to us. In it is the story of a couture seamstress in a concentration camp who customised her fellow inmates' prison uniforms and made headdresses and hats out of scraps of material. It reminds me of another Second World War story of a group of young Girl Guides interned in Changi Prison in Singapore after the invasion, who decided to sew a beautiful quilt for their Girl Guiding leader as a gift. They used pieces of fabric torn from clothes and uniforms, creating a rosette pattern. The centre of each rosette has a name embroidered into it. It's incredibly beautiful. The piece now hangs in the Imperial War Museum in London. We turn to art, even in the most horrific of times. Perhaps it is then that we need it more than ever, to remind us of what there is to live for.

Sonia shows me around the rest of her home. She uses the house to photograph artwork she is selling at the gallery, so that potential customers can see it in a home context. Sonia calls herself a compulsive curator. She loves moving the works around. She understands that some people do struggle with knowing how to display art, especially if they have only seen it in a gallery setting. As we walk through the rooms, she tells me where she thinks she'll move the pieces to next and what other pieces she's got her eye on that may work in the house. They have only been there for six months, and she's enjoying playing around with it.

The subject of having the confidence to just play comes up yet again. She tells me that we take everything so seriously, but it's fine to just try a piece out on a wall; if you don't love it there, you can just move it. Of course, buying a more expensive piece does take thought. With some clients, she goes to visit their homes so they can work out together where a piece they are considering might go.

I ask her what advice she would give if people don't know where to start when it comes to hanging art.

'The first thing to remember is: just because you spend some money on it and perhaps consider it to be "important", that doesn't mean it has to be front and centre in the middle of a wall or above your fireplace. It's okay for it not to be centre stage; it could quietly be in an alcove. It's okay for it to *cwtch** up somewhere, next to another piece. Sometimes it might need something else to give it context.'

*A Welsh word that doesn't really exist in English – similar to snuggle.

In Sonia's calm, light bedroom, she has a very small Sam Lock painting, in gold, taupe and cream tones. It sits on an otherwise vast and empty wall, to the right of her bed, rather than centrally. It is counter to what many would think of as the 'right' way to hang a piece of art. But it has created the exact feel Sonia wanted. It is tranquil and reflects the feeling of serenity she wanted in the room, with all that negative space.

Using shelves is another great way to play with art and display, she tells me. Narrow shelves mean you can curate pictures and paintings next to found objects, ceramics, glassware and personal objects. There is no fear about putting holes in walls and no problem with shifting items around when you get bored or feel like changing things with the seasons.

As we walk around, Sonia tells me that in her previous home, which she lived in for seventeen years, she had a desk set up under the stairs and above her desk was a wall covered in family photographs. 'I loved to work feeling surrounded by all my people,' she tells me. The rest of the house was carefully curated with artworks and yet when people would come over, they'd walk past her desk on the way to the kitchen and people would stop and want to spend time there. Everyone was drawn to it. We love to see what other people feel is important to them.

Kemi's and Sonia's homes are very different in many ways, but both women have created something with deep personal connection to the objects and decoration within them, as well as carefully curating the spaces to reflect their aesthetic tastes. Kemi in her attention to colour and pattern, moments of surprise and celebration of ancestry. Sonia in her deep appreciation for art, for the moments in time they represent and the carefully chosen objects that connect her to her memories. Both are incredibly joyful homes in their own way.

On the chest of drawers in Sonia's bedroom, among the items her daughters have given her over the years, sits a small, square black-and-white photo. The surround of the photo is white, and at the bottom a large nappy pin has been stuck though it. The photo is of a baby girl, lying on a blanket, the shadow of a woman across her. The baby is Sonia. Her birth mother, who had her adopted at three months, took that photo just before she said goodbye to her. The day she gave Sonia away, she removed the pin from her nappy to keep with her. When they met for the first time when Sonia was thirty, her birth mother gave her the nappy pin, along with the negatives for the photo – a tangible reminder that her birth mother had not wanted to forget. Sonia printed the photo herself and placed the pin in the bottom. It sits alongside the other objects that connect her to her family. A simple display that represents the past, the present and the future. I think it might be the most beautiful piece of art in the whole house.

On my return from Wales, I attend to a job I have been meaning to do for years. Among the items I kept of Mum's belongings is a large watercolour painting of irises – my mum's favourite flowers. She bought the painting while we were visiting my dad when he was working in the US. I remember it in every house we lived in. It is present in the background of countless birthday celebration and Christmas photos. It has been unframed and shoved beside my wardrobe for years. I pull it out and take it to the picture framer. A few weeks later, it is up in my bedroom. Looking at it, I feel so connected to my mum that I now understand why I put it off for so long. Its large, beautiful presence is as much her as a photo of her would be. Perhaps even more so. I think of how my daughter will, over time, begin to associate it with me. My past and my future converging in a way that feels rare. My mother died long before my children were born. There is an unfathomable chasm between them that is hard to bridge. Perhaps it is objects like these that can help to bridge that gap.

Our desire for beauty is perhaps our desire for connection above all else. Connection to our pasts and to those we love. Our need to adorn our homes, to make them more than just a box or shelter, is perhaps connected to our desire to live beyond the immediate moment. We can be reminded that we are not alone, that we have ancestors and pasts, and we have futures, too. And they are all interconnected.

Chapter Eight: The Living Home

Somerset, and Mooroolbark, Melbourne

The question about whether I should write about gardens in a book about the home went round in my head for a long time. But it was the homeowners themselves who answered this question for me. So many had a lot to say, unprompted, about their gardens, unable to unlink them from the idea of home. It seemed I didn't have much choice in the matter. I had my own reasons for actively avoiding the topic, but perhaps it was time to face up to them.

*

It is summer, and the hydrangea bushes are bursting over the front fence and onto the path. One has already gone from deep blue-purple to a faded violet, and the other from a dark, vibrant pink to dusky. There aren't many roses this year, which I assume is because I haven't pruned the bushes the way I am supposed to. Hazel trees stick up in various places, and although I did recently get rid of some of the self-seeded sycamores, I can see that various new ones have sprung up, their roots pushing through the crack between the house and the foundations. The beds are all entirely covered with various weeds, as well as between the irregular paving stones. Some are flowering, attractive and wild. Others not so much.

The back garden is more chaotic. I have a fairly healthy apple tree, planted after I found it at a supermarket for £1.50 eight years ago, and a few other plants and trees that I have randomly stuck in the ground over the years, but most people would probably draw in a deep breath at the sight of it. When I mention this to friends, they shrug their shoulders and say, 'Oh well, not everyone is into gardening.' But the truth is, when I look at my dismal attempts at gardening I feel deeply ashamed.

I grew up in the most magical garden. One that was as much 'home' as the house. I'm lucky enough to have this small patch of land in this impossibly large city, and I know the garden would give me so much if I could just devote a little time and effort to it. But on the long to-do list of being a parent and unpaid carer, writing, earning a living and running a household, the garden is forever slipping to the bottom.

'The garden has a language all to itself, one of soil quality and life cycles, shade and sun, drainage, seedlings, snails and a hundred other mysterious inner workings.'

When I walked through my childhood garden again at Badgers Wood, I marvelled at the size and the sheer amount of effort it must have taken for my parents to keep it up. Because unlike other aspects of a home, which might, aside from tidying and cleaning, require very little maintenance for years at a time, gardens require a yearly round of effort in order to reap the rewards they have to offer. The garden has a language all to itself, one of soil quality and life cycles, shade and sun, drainage, seedlings, snails and a hundred other mysterious inner workings that I hear snippets of on Gardeners' Question Time but have not ever had quite the headspace to delve into very deeply.

Gazing out onto my own scraggly green patch, the feelings it invokes in me also answers the question of whether or not gardens need to be included in a book about homes. If the garden didn't mean much to me, I could simply reduce it entirely to lawn and pay the teenager next door to keep it under control. Either that or replace it with Astroturf, which a number of people have suggested. But the thought of doing either of those things is horrifying to me, much like living in an empty white house with no personal items would. I decide to listen to that instinct and explore the idea of what role our gardens might play for us in our homes. Even if it does mean I may confront a few difficult home truths about myself.

When I visited Kate Sessions in Chapter Three, the garden came up in conversation almost immediately. I remembered Kate's sweet, small garden in London and then saw the vast acre she now has her hands on in Yorkshire. It is on the scale of my childhood garden, stretching far back and bordering onto a field. It's walled and has a small orchard, with daffodils springing up in clusters. Tulips burst out in bright oranges and yellows, and right at the very back lies a disused menage, where the previous owners worked their horses. She plans on turning it into a wildflower meadow in time, but for now it's a spot for football and rounders with the kids.

She tells me she had a lot of affection for her London garden, but this is different. She feels able to (quite literally) put roots down in a way that she perhaps felt a little too tentative to do in the London garden, even though they didn't have plans to leave. The garden here in Yorkshire has been lovingly looked after over the years, even as the house itself became run down. It felt, she tells me, like a large responsibility to take charge of it. Far more so than the house itself.

Kate grew up in nearby York and they had a fairly decent-sized garden for the medieval city, though not nearly as large as this. Kate's mother had been an avid gardener and, like my own, also died quite young, while Kate was still in her twenties. She tells me that moving back to Yorkshire and finding this garden, close to the hills that her mother adored and where her grave now lies, is the first time she has really allowed herself to fully embrace gardening.

'When I put my hands in the soil here,' she tells me, 'it's like I can feel her. I feel connected to her. Maybe that's why I wasn't ready to do it earlier.' She shakes her head as if I might think she's mad, but Kate has just articulated something that I have never been able to put my finger on. Perhaps it's easier for me to pour time and energy into the inside of my home, because doing so in the garden might just open up a flood of feelings I might not be able to stop. Visiting the garden at Badgers Wood only confirmed that.

When I think of my mother, I think of her in that garden. I think of her in floaty summer dresses and wide-brimmed hats or gumboots, cords and woollen jumpers. She is standing with her hands on her hips, examining some bit of the garden; she is pulling up weeds, or else she is chatting with friends under the pergola with wine in hand.

In Melbourne, while staying with my friend Georgie, her father, Philip, popped by to have a cup of tea. Philip is a strong presence in my childhood memories. He was a college lecturer so was always around a lot on the weekends and long summer holidays. I told him I was writing about Bickleigh Vale and I wanted to hear his memories and thoughts of the place. It's been thirty years since Philip and Georgie's mother divorced and their house was sold.

'I was the one who really loved the garden,' he tells me. 'I spent hours and hours out there. It was a lot of work, but I loved doing it. And it's how I became so friendly with your mum and everyone else on the street.' Philip, who had been born and raised in Shropshire, seemed to fit perfectly into this enclave built by Edna Walling in my memory. But what also drew them to Bickleigh Vale was the community. They had the idea that this idyll that Walling had created might give them exactly what they needed to raise their daughters. And it did. Although the marriage eventually ended, the garden, and the community around it, had brought them all a lot of happiness.

I think about how these gardens have linked us all. That thirty years later, Philip, along with Georgie, Lucy, Em and all their parents are like family to me. It was more than just being neighbours. The gardens themselves attracted specific people to them, just as they had when Edna Walling designed and built the original cottages. Her unique blend of landscape design and conservation meant that those who lived there did so knowing they had a responsibility to the village community. It was, after all, not just a street of manicured gardens imposed on the landscape, like most suburbs. It was an example of how residential areas can be managed in a way that supported the natural, local environment. But that management took effort. And that effort brought people together.

Somerset

Back in England, I am driving west very early one morning to a village in Somerset, just south of Bath. It's a gloriously sunny and warm day, with no signs of the wet summer still to come our way. I drive through the village a couple of times before I spot the house and park up. The Bath-stone house sits close to the road, and I can see the garden already, climbing up the hillside. This is the home of Marchelle Farrell and her family, who moved here three and a half years ago from Oxford. Marchelle greets me and we take our coffee out onto the decking. I have a view over the lower garden, a wildflower meadow, and the fields and woods beyond. The only noises are the sheep bleating nearby and the occasional car coming out of the village. It is enchanting.

Marchelle tells me they had been thinking about moving for a while, but in the end it happened quite suddenly. Her husband Oli, an NHS cardiologist, was offered a job in Bath and they had two months to make the move happen. They assumed they would have to rent but when they saw this place, they knew it was exactly what they wanted. 'I fell in love with the garden, really,' Marchelle says, 'not so much the house.'

Marchelle, originally from Trinidad, had spent two decades as an NHS psychiatrist and psychotherapist, training and working with extremely complex patients. Their two children were still young and Marchelle had been feeling very burnt out. Over the previous few years, she had been exploring her interest in plants and flexing her writing muscles for the first time since she was young. Part of what drove the move was a need for her to root herself, to find a connection to the land she was on, to develop a relationship with the place – something she felt had been missing in their urban home in Oxford. She was also driven by a desire to give her children the best

chance possible in life. From her work as a psychiatrist, she knew too well the risks her children were facing. Black men, specifically first generation British-born, of Caribbean descent, raised in urban areas, were at the highest risk of anyone in the UK for receiving a diagnosis of schizophrenia. The number reduced significantly for those raised in the countryside. The moment she gave birth to her son, she could not get the statistics out of her mind.

'There is something about the topography of [this] place that really reminds me of the home my parents bought [in Trinidad] when I was a teenager. A house perched on this steep slope, with a lot of terracing – not a traditional flat lawn in sight. It felt so familiar. I think I saw something of what this place could become with us here. I think I was projecting something onto the space without perhaps realising it.'

The family moved in late 2019, with no idea just how important the garden would become. Marchelle, whose job is highly specialised, did not immediately have a job to go to and planned to have a career break while they settled in. 'I was personally in a lot of turmoil,' Marchelle tells me. 'I'd given up a career that had been my identity. You are a doctor. There is a breaking yourself down and a building yourself up that happens in medical training, so breaking free from that is very hard.' But it turned out to be strangely well timed.

When the pandemic hit in March 2020, Oli, whose speciality is cardiology, was the youngest and healthiest member of his team and so was put on the frontline. It was an extremely traumatic time, and though Marchelle's first instinct during the crisis was to go back to work, she decided in the end that it would be impossible. The kids were very young, Oli's parents were shielding completely and Oli himself was at high risk every single day. It made sense for her to be at home with the children and give Oli the support he needed.

Oli was asked to work more nights, and that meant he was around more during the daytime to share some of the care of the kids. Marchelle, who was alone with the children most of the time, began to take a couple of hours each day to garden alone. That summer, after George Floyd's murder, latent memories of a lifetime of racist experiences came to the surface. It was there, with her hands in the soil, that she began to feel she could process what was happening in this immense year.

'In all my training, we spent all this time thinking about relationships, but we never really thought about relationships with place. And I was having such a profound response to this place.'

Marchelle tells me that there is a theory in psychotherapy of the 'development of thinking'. When a baby is born, its brain is underdeveloped, and how it begins to learn is in a dynamic with a maternal, or caregiver's, mind. A baby has proto-thoughts, which are really feelings (I'm cold, I'm hungry, I'm uncomfortable), which they can't make any sense of, so they communicate by crying. The caregiver helps them to make sense of those feelings by responding to this communication. As that co-regulation happens over and over again, the baby begins to understand and identify what is hunger, what is tired, what is cold, and the feelings become less terrifying. The baby begins to make sense of things, and to think.

'I was having all these massive feelings and I felt as though I was pouring them into the garden. Through working in the garden, being with the plants, I would start having coherent thoughts that I could then actually talk about and write about.'

'It felt like that was what the garden was doing for me,' she says. 'I was having all these massive feelings and I felt as though I was pouring them into the garden. Through working in the garden, being with the plants, I would start having coherent thoughts that I could then actually talk about and write about.'

I'm fascinated by this comparison and I want to understand it more. I ask Marchelle what she thinks the benefits of gardening are from a psychiatric perspective.

'There is this terribly shallow stuff which you see thrown about the internet – "Oh, gardening is good for your mental health. It increases serotonin!" and yes, I suppose that's true in a way, that gardening is "good for us". But really, what I believe is that we have, as humans, become so detached from the fact that we are animals, who are part of the natural world. We have built structures and cities to be our habitats, we are detached from nature and as a result we have gone a bit mad as a species.'

It's not all about experiencing good feelings. Being an animal in nature will bring all the feelings. 'Being in the muddy, bare garden, in the middle of winter, having just turned my life upside down, brought up a lot of old feelings,' Marchelle says with a laugh. 'It brought up feelings around times when I felt infertile and impotent and unsure, and when I didn't know what was coming next. I was looking for signs of hope and not seeing them immediately in the bare soil. That is the full, rich tapestry of life.'

My thoughts stray back to Kate's explanation of what happens to her when she has her hands in the soil of her Yorkshire garden. How she is connecting with her mother in a profound way. These are not all happy feelings, but it is a deeply needed connection.

I think of all the other homeowners who spontaneously began talking with me about their gardens. People who I hadn't previously realised had such a strong sense of connection to them. In Chapter Two in Cornwall, Rebecca Proctor's garden is walled and sheltered from the harsh north winds. It's an irreplaceable oasis that is one of the main reasons they have never left. Up in Northumberland, Caro Giles and her daughters are almost as deeply attached to their allotment as they are to the house.

Early on the morning I stayed, the Giles girls took me around the corner to see their allotment. Without a back garden, this patch of rented land a street away has been an extension of their home during a very difficult few years of lockdowns, poor health and increasingly complex needs. The girls see the allotment as part of their home, so for two of them particularly, it is a very safe space to be in. It's the size of a large suburban garden and has established fruit trees, lots of flowers, some lawn and a few beds of vegetables. Caro's eldest showed me the pond she built herself and the tadpoles and frogs that live in it. Caro told me that the pond is her happy place, where she can totally relax. There are few places in the world where she can feel that way. The youngest two bounced on the trampoline, while Caro and I walked around. It was utterly beautiful. A little bit of magic tucked away behind a row of terraced houses. In 2021, when her eldest daughter was extremely unwell and barely able to leave the house, this was the one place they could come. Unable to ever leave her daughter alone, Caro would run around the allotment in circles to get some exercise. You have to find some freedom anyway you can, she told me. And this allotment meant a safe way of doing that for all of them.

Every time the garden is brought up in conversations, I hear the same themes repeated. Safety, solace, time, patience, connection. It's as though gardens, rooted in the natural world, unable to be so fully controlled as the houses themselves, become extensions of our human selves. Living and breathing, just as we are, they can hold our emotions in ways that other areas of our homes cannot. But equally, they can be overwhelming, because of the effort and attention they demand from us.

Marchelle explains that she sees gardening as a relationship. It's a dialogue and we have to learn to listen. She tells me it's no good to decide that you simply want something to look a very specific way and try to bend it to your will. The garden will communicate with you about what works and what doesn't, and you have to pay attention. Marchelle's training as a psychotherapist was all about paying attention. So much of what patients communicate is not in words, she tells me. It's about how they say it, what they don't say, what their body is telling her. She learned to attune carefully to her own physical, somatic responses in the therapy room and somehow articulate that back to the patient in words. Perhaps, she says, she had some of those skills already, and that might be why she was attracted to the work, but certainly all those years of training and working with patients had her listening carefully and paying close attention. She uses the same skills in her garden.

She walks me around her garden and shows me where she began and how it has changed since they arrived. Outside the back doors there is a patio and seating area, and the garden rises up the hill beyond it. Stone terracing creates beds that at this point in midsummer are overflowing with flowers and plants, an abundant riot of colour and growth. A stream runs throughout the garden, largely hidden at the moment due to the rich summer growth. It's a tributary of an ancient stream that was a site of pilgrimage, known for its healing properties. In winter, Marchelle tells me, when much of the garden has retreated to a dormant state, the stream is such an important part of the garden. It is visible and audible evidence that the garden is still very much alive, and the sound of it can be heard throughout the house if you open any window.

At the top of the terracing, there is a back gate that leads out onto the road and into the village. One of the things that makes this garden so unique is that much of the garden, rather than being entirely behind the house, runs alongside it, parallel to the road, separated from it by a high beech hedge. This gate is how they enter the house, every time they come and go. Oli cycles in to the hospital, and the bike shed sits up by this gate. The school run is taken this way, too. That way, the garden is used multiple times a day, without even having to think about it. We stand at the top under a huge ash tree, looking down through the lush garden to the house at the bottom, the sheep-dotted paddock rising up behind it, with woods beyond.

'I come in from the school run and the first thing I see is this view,' Marchelle tells me. 'It's like taking a deep breath.'

I think of Rebecca Proctor's walled garden in Cornwall and how it provides the same. Entirely at the front of the house, you have to be in the garden in order to leave the house. It naturally makes the garden part of your day, rather than separate from it. I think about how this differs from the way so many people experience their gardens – the ones lucky enough to have them. In the winter I know I can go a long period of time without going out the back at all.

We walk back down the winding path and behind the house, where Marchelle has installed some beds for growing vegetables. Colourful sweet peas climb up poles, kale is growing thickly under protective fabric and her chickens peck their way among the grass between the beds. Beyond this are some fruit trees and then the lower part of the garden that has been given over to wildflowers. It was a pristine lawn when they moved in, and as part of Marchelle's ethos to listen, she knew she wanted to allow this part of the garden to be less controlled. The long grasses are dotted through with poppies, cornflowers and daisies. A path has formed, which leads to the hedgerows that border the property, and a bench sits by the stream as it makes its way out of the garden and into the field beyond.

'Just like birds weave their nests, we can shape our home environments in ways that regulate our nervous system.'

As we walk, we talk about the idea of human habitats. 'We forget that our built environments are our habitats,' she tells me. 'Just like birds weave their nests, we can shape our home environments in ways that regulate our nervous system. But we are so disconnected from that idea. That's not how we approach our homes.' Instead, we get stuck inside our heads and forget about our bodies. 'Our body is our first home,' Marchelle says, and we don't always have a comfortable relationship with it. 'I think that a lot of society's ills come from this disconnection from our bodies.' As a medical doctor, psychiatrist and psychotherapist, Marchelle has treated some extremely complex people, so I don't doubt that she knows what she is talking about. This disconnection is also how we have got into the deep trouble we are in with our natural environment. Centuries of taking, of colonialism, of ignoring indigenous wisdom and constantly imposing our will on the planet has led to a crisis. But, like me, Marchelle is hopeful and doesn't believe humans are only a toxic burden on our planet. We have the capacity as humans to live in harmony with it, just as other animals do. But we need to listen to it. This garden, on a small scale, feels like an example of how we can thrive in our relationship with the land.

In Edna Walling's later years, she turned her back on most of the European plants she used in her earlier gardens. She was drawn instead to native plants, studying and writing about the Australian roadside landscape and what can be learned about conserving the natural environment while living side by side with it. But I had grown up in one of her hybrid gardens – one that felt both Australian and English at the same time. It is one of the reasons I think I have always felt a little bit at home in this country. It's as if the house and garden I grew up in somehow permeated me and I carry them with me always.

*

After I visit Kate in Yorkshire in early spring, her words about connecting with her mother through the garden ring in my ears. Back in my own garden, I take a deep breath and look at the dahlia tubers dumped at my feet, along with the packets of seeds – forget-me-nots and foxgloves – plants that grew in abundance at Badgers Wood. Jane, my next-door neighbour, spots me and waves hello. She and her husband moved in the same year as me; their kids are younger than mine. I always marvel at what Jane manages to do in the garden. Bright bulbs push up each spring and vegetables in late summer. When I have asked her about it in the past she has just shrugged and laughed, and said she has no idea what she's doing, just making it up as she goes along.

I tell her now that I am doing some planting and ask if she knows if I can just sow the seeds straight into the ground. Will it work? I can't grow seedlings indoors, as my son plays with any soil he can get his hands on. And pots are not safe either, not since the time I found him hurling them around and squealing in delight as they smashed and scattered on the patio.

Jane shrugs and says she's not sure, but when she sees what I've chosen she turns her back for a moment and then comes back to the fence with pots. They are overflowing with forget-me-nots, that familiar tiny blue flower that was scattered across my childhood garden. She holds them over the fence. 'Take them! I'm overrun. I planted them last year. They self-seed and they're everywhere now,' she says with a laugh. 'Just dig a hole and stick them in.'

This is something a number of people have told me now. Don't overthink it, just stick some plants in the ground and see what happens. It turns out gardening is more about watching and listening than knowing. Karen Haller, in our conversation around colour (see page 92), had waved a hand at her living room, which I could see through Zoom; she had laughed and said, 'I'm much more into the garden now than my house.' She didn't know anything much about gardening; she just bought things and tried them out. Now she spends a couple of hours a day out there.

The forget-me-nots take and I enjoy the sight of the tiny flowers for weeks before they retreat to healthy, plump green plants. The dahlias begin to push up fast and before long I have a plant so heavy with flowers it collapses in a storm. I add some flowering chives on Kate's recommendation, and they seem to love the spot. The nettles keep coming back and I fail to stay completely on top of them, but when I look around the garden I see so much life, bursting out of every corner. It's messy and not well thought out, but it is alive.

It is around this time that I am reading Alice Vincent's book *Why Women Grow*. Curled up in bed one weekend morning drinking tea, surrounded by gardening books, including one I ordered from Australia about Edna Walling, I read the closing pages of what Vincent concludes from all the conversations she's had walking in gardens with the women who planted them. I'm struck by how her search is a parallel one to mine with homes.

'A foxglove growing out of my own soil, in this very moment, connects me on some level to all the foxgloves my mother grew, in a way that is more vivid than a picture of her, or even a chair she used to sit on.'

One observation seems to stand out, cutting straight to what I know to be a deep personal truth. 'Women grow because raising a garden can forge connective tissue to something lost.' In that one sentence I can see the complexities of why I both yearn for and avoid my garden. Perhaps the inside of my house has been a safer, more controlled space where I can connect to what has been lost. But in the living, breathing garden, that connection is both in the present and the past at the same time. A foxglove growing out of my own soil, in this very moment, connects me on some level to all the foxgloves my mother grew, in a way that is more vivid than a picture of her, or even a chair she used to sit on.

Later in the summer, a large envelope falls onto the doormat. Lucy's mother, Rae, has recently died after a long illness with Alzheimer's. I couldn't get to Australia to attend the memorial, but Dad was able to go and has sent me a copy of a book that Lucy has told me about. Rae was diagnosed with Alzheimer's in 2008, and in 2015, knowing that the illness was now progressing at speed, she sat down to write her life story. It feels especially poignant given that Rae had lost so much in the last years of her illness, that she had the foresight and the courage to do this for her family and friends before it was too late. She writes beautifully about her childhood, her parents and her siblings. She writes about her relationship with her husband, David, and her three children and her grandchildren, whom she adored. But a huge amount of the book is about her gardens. Her childhood garden and the garden in her first home with David. She writes about Bickleigh Vale and the efforts made to have the gardens protected and open to the public, and the sense of community that fostered. Photographs of all her gardens and her favourite flowers are peppered throughout. But most poignantly of all, she writes about her last garden in Healesville, how she planned and planted the garden, her designs heavily influenced by Edna Walling. She writes about what that garden gave her, just as she was losing so much. 'What a joy my garden is to me, and such a solace. I love walking around it – smelling, weeding, wandering, walking.' At a time when she was struggling with so much, she was highly aware of the beauty around her, that she could still access it, just outside in her garden. Her words make me think more about the kind of impact growing up in one of Edna Walling's gardens has had on me.

*

Mooroolbark, Melbourne

The garden at Badgers Wood is designed almost as a series of rooms. You can't take in the garden all at once, and there are constant surprises as you walk around it. Stone steps lead from the back of the house down to a lawn, and beyond it there are a few directions you can go in. The pergola, weighted down with years of growth, leads to a pond and a trio of trees, which my parents planted for me and my brothers. Another path between shrubs and trees leads to the lower part of the garden where I, when I visit, am surprised to see the same swing set that my parents installed still stands (it has a new seat and ropes). Here, you are completely out of sight of the house, and this was where my friends and I would come to play away from prying adult eyes. Here, you could be anywhere in the world in your imagination.

A vast golden wych elm stands in this lower part of the garden. It is larger than I remember even as a child. Memories flood in as I see it, of painting outdoors, of picnics and playing with tiny toys in its tree roots. It was the Magic Faraway Tree, grown as if by enchantment from the pages of my favourite book. The leaves are a pale lime green, and it stretches to what looks like about three storeys high, maybe more. In the autumn the leaves go an almost pure golden colour before a rich orange and then brown.

Later, my friend Toby, who has a deep interest in trees, tells me he has gone to a Bickleigh Vale open garden day especially to see that tree. It strikes me then that I have not seen one anywhere else that I can remember. Then I realise that although the golden wych elm is

the only elm native to England, Dutch elm disease has almost wiped them out here. Yet there one stands, in my childhood garden in Australia, while almost all of its English predecessors are gone.

It is in my childhood garden, with its connection to two continents, native soil and ghost gums, alongside the settler plants of agapanthus, crab apples and elms, that I see how I have made a home for my children that straddles both those places, too. We are a complex family. Divorce and disability mean that I decided long ago that London is where we will stay, even if my heart often yearns to be in Melbourne.

It is in the garden that these influences all converge, and it is in our London garden that I am reminded that I am both at home and not at home all at once. Perhaps it is time to stop avoiding the garden. Perhaps it is time to put my hands in the soil and plant a gum tree in my English garden.

Conclusion: The Good-enough Home

When my mother died she left behind a house filled with her things. There was the beautiful and the precious: antique furniture, some art, a Wedgwood dinner set. And there was the mundane: Tupperware, spice jars, countless wooden spoons, my old school blazer, which I hadn't known she'd kept. Her suicide was both completely unexpected and not a surprise at all. I flew back from London, where I had just moved weeks earlier; my eldest brother Ash from the US where he lived and worked; my brother Pip from a holiday he had been on. We all convened in my mother's house, which she had owned for five years. I had lived there for three of those while I was at university. None of us was particularly attached to this house. It was a contemporary build on a small suburban block in a pretty part of Melbourne. It had been the right choice for her – it was low maintenance and it was not isolated – but it had not felt like a home to any of us. It had perhaps been too coloured by the challenges that had led our mother to buy it.

My mother's accountant, Newell, who was friendly with both of our parents so we knew him well, read us the will as we sat among her things in the living room. There were no surprises. My mother was nothing if not organised and fair. She specified a few items for each of us. Jewellery and clothing for me; a few bits of antique furniture for my brothers. The rest of her things were to be divided up in thirds. Newell explained that this meant, by law, it had to be exactly in thirds. So our job that day was to decide what we would each take, so that he could have everything valued. Then, he would take that into account when he split up the money that she had left behind. It had to be exactly in thirds in terms of financial value. And it couldn't wait. Ash had to get back to work in Arizona. I had a job and a room in a flat in London I was already paying rent on. It had to be done before we were scattered. Newell suggested a method to make it go as smoothly as possible. We were each given sheets of stickers of coloured dots. Mine were red. We were to put a sticker on the things we wanted, and after we were finished he would have everything valued and marked according to who was taking it. Anything without

Conclusion

a sticker would also need to be valued but would be donated to charity. Mum had set money aside for all this to be taken care of, alongside her funeral and any other legal costs. Like I said, she was very organised.

It was an odd experience. I had just turned twenty-two and I was faced with a lifetime of objects. What was important? What could be discarded? Mum had been dead less than ten days and I felt ill-equipped to make these choices. How would I know if I was making the right decision? My brothers and I wandered around saying things like, 'You should have that,' and, 'Nah, I never really liked that.' It felt like the antithesis of every post-funeral, will-reading scene I'd ever read or seen on film. We weren't fighting over anything. In fact, we were each trying to encourage the others to take more. There were a few items I felt certain about that I was very happy to put my red sticker on. The iris painting, the Quaker armchair, the black-and-white photo of my mother in front of Badgers Wood. But, mostly, I walked around in a daze, putting my dots on random things that my brothers didn't want. It felt unreal. And, in some ways, it was.

I lived in a small double room in a shared house with four others just off the Hackney Road in East London. It had a bed and a pine wardrobe and dresser in it and barely any floor space. I worked in a photography studio for £200 a week and more than half that went on my rent. I would not be taking a Wedgwood dinner set to London. I couldn't yet picture a day when I would have the home or the inclination for a dinner set. Ash and I decided together, since we both lived abroad, that we would put our share into a storage container for the time being. So after the valuation, when we had gone back to our respective countries, everything with a yellow or red sticker would be packed by a moving company into a shipping container and deposited in a distant warehouse. The day went by in a haze. When I got on a plane the following week, I could not remember a single thing I had put a sticker on.

A year later, on a visit home, I paid to have the container emptied and laid out in the warehouse. It was not the kind of storage where you can wander in and browse around. It was cheaper, long-term storage where everything was packed in as if it was about to go in a cargo ship and be stuck in a warehouse reminiscent of the one in the last scene in Raiders of the Lost Ark. I had booked it weeks earlier, thinking that I could do a bit of sorting out, get rid of some more things.

The moment I saw it all spread out across a warehouse floor – boxes, chairs, sideboards and bed frames – I sat down and cried. I was looking at the remnants of home. In this warehouse on an industrial park on the outskirts of the city, my whole life, and my mother's, was strewn across concrete. I had been unprepared for seeing it all out of context, outside of a house. I had been expecting to see stuff, but what I saw instead was a home that no longer existed. Overwhelmed, I picked through the boxes and found some small items. A few pictures, some leather boots, a wool scarf, some trinkets. I had just moved out of my London flat and was about to move to New York, so I couldn't take much. Drained, and having achieved almost nothing, I left. It was perhaps the moment when I really understood that I no longer had a home.

I made a couple of visits to it over the years, each time sending a few more of the larger pieces off to charity, but mostly I left feeling flat, untethered and as if I no longer belonged anywhere. As long as my mother's and my own childhood belongings remained locked in a warehouse with nowhere to send them, I was in a kind of limbo. I called both London and Melbourne home. But without my mother, without that solid place to return to, did I have a home at all?

It was fifteen years after she died and the year that I got divorced that I finally emptied that shipping container. I had become highly aware, through the process of separation, that I was my children's home now. I had managed to hang on to our house in the divorce, thanks

'My home, just like all the homes I have had the privilege of walking through during the course of writing this book, is an amalgamation of my past, present and future.'

largely to my mother and the deposit I had gained from my share of the sale of her house. She was the reason I could give my children a home. There may not have been a time when she and my children were alive at the same time, but there was a link that ran through me to them. I whittled that shipping container down to a single pallet of items to be shipped to London. Just the most precious things. And I let the rest go. The items I took are now intermingled with things I have collected over the past twenty-three years since I left Melbourne.

My home, just like all the homes I have had the privilege of walking through during the course of writing this book, is an amalgamation of my past, present and future. It is something that gives me a feeling of enormous safety and respite, but it is so much more than that, too. From its hole in the kitchen ceiling, to the damaged bathroom floor, it is far from perfect. Far from some kind of ideal. It's beautiful and a bit of a mess. But it is also all mine.

When I look back at how I used to scoff at the idea of being an interiors photographer, I think about how little I understood about how and why the aesthetics of our homes matter so much to us. They are intimate and protective. They are places to explore our passions and interests. Places we can play and be ourselves.

But they are also places that do not have to be perfect. They don't have to be finished or 'done'. As important as our homes are, they just need to be good enough. What good enough is to each of us is a question that only we alone can answer. It can't be found here in this book, or in any other. But one thing I feel more strongly about than ever is that thinking deeply about our homes matters. Paying attention to how we feel in them, to how we respond to colour, objects, flow and space, and then acting on those feelings, appreciating and perhaps bringing in more of what makes us feel good, is hugely important. It allows our inner selves to be reflected and projected onto our homes.

As Karen Haller pointed out to me, constantly looking for outward validation, following trends and surrounding ourselves with things we think we should want is a futile, never-ending loop that will only leave us dissatisfied and put pressure on us to consume. Satisfaction, though, can be found in the process of discovery and in playing with our homes.

The perfect home does not exist. There is no perfect size, layout, colour, item of furniture, number of rooms or outdoor space. But we all deserve a home that meets the needs of every person who lives there, no matter whether it's owned or rented, or we live there as a social tenant. No matter how much we earn, no matter our background.

Through my conversations with social workers, psychologists and those working with some of the most marginalised people in our society, I've tried to imagine just what would be possible if the starting point for all of us was a home that we felt safe in, that we could afford and that made us feel good. It would not make all our other problems disappear. But it could provide us with a stable base to step out from. Somewhere to feel protected and secure when the world around us sometimes feels anything but. A place where we could feel a little in control. That, to me, would be a good-enough home. And every single one of us deserves that.

Endnotes

p. 35
Greg Stevenson, *The 1930s Home* (London: Shire Library, 2009).

p. 42
'London's richest and poorest boroughs: The average incomes in 2022 where you live', thelondonpress.uk, 14 March 2022: https://thelondonpress.
uk/2022/03/14/londons-richest-and-poorest-boroughs-the-average-incomes-in-2022-where-you-live/?utm_content=cmp-true

Rupert Jones, 'House price growth outstrips wages in 90% of England and Wales', *Guardian*, 23 March 2022: https://www.theguardian.com/money/2022/mar/23/house-price-growth-outstrips-wages-england-wales

p. 48
Olivia Heath, 'This is the average size home in England and Wales – and how it compares to the EU & USA', *House Beautiful*, 12 October 2017: https://www.housebeautiful.com/uk/lifestyle/property/news/a2590/average-uk-property-size-comparison/

p. 49
Average house size Australia: How many square metres is standard?' *Better Homes and Gardens*, 11 August 2020: https://www.bhg.com.au/average-house-size-australia-how-many-square-metres-is-standard

Karen Chen, 'The big idea behind the "tiny house" movement', *Financial Times*, 1 May 2020: https://www.ft.com/content/6276e4b2-41c6-11ea-a879-e56a76ed3e8a

p. 49
Overcrowding, Shelter: https://england.shelter.org.uk/professional_resources/legal/housing_conditions/overcrowding

Ethnicity facts and figures: Overcrowded households, Gov.uk: https://www.ethnicity-facts-figures.service.gov.uk/housing/housing-conditions/overcrowded-households/latest

'Full house? How overcrowded housing affects families', Shelter report, 2005: https://assets.ctfassets.net/6sxvmndnpn0s/6dU8FFbZ6RnSk6DbnDOMHb/61e30884aff47a789891b2dce54fcbc7 /Full_house_overcrowding_effects.pdf

p. 54
Sarah Susanka, *The Not So Big House* (Newtown: Taunton Press, 1998).

p. 76
Deyan Sudjic, *The Language of Things* (London: Penguin, 2008), p.21.

Ibid., p.21.

p. 82
'How Much Do Our Wardrobes Cost to the Environment?' World Bank, 23 September 2019: https://www.worldbank.org/en/news/feature/2019/09/23/costo-moda-medio-ambiente

Alain de Botton, *Status Anxiety* (London: Hamish Hamilton, 2004).

p. 94
Karen Haller, *The Little Book of Colour: How to Use the Psychology of Colour to Transform Your Life* (London: Penguin Life, 2019), p. 10.

Ibid., p. 11.

p. 95
Ibid., p.180.

Rachel Kurzius, 'HGTV is making our homes boring and us sad, one study says', *Washington Post*, 7 July 2023: https://www.washingtonpost.com/home/2023/07/07/hgtv-makes-homes-boring-sad/

p. 124
'Housing crisis affects estimated 8.4 million in England – research', BBC, 23 September 2019: https://www.bbc.co.uk/news/uk-49787913

Index of Private Housing Rental Prices, UK: May 2023, Office for National Statistics: https://www.ons.gov.uk/economy/inflationandpriceindices/bulletins/

'New insights into the rental market', Australian Bureau of Statistics, 24 April 2023: https://www.abs.gov.au/statistics/detailed-methodology-information/information-papers/new-insights-rental-market

'1 in 7 people in England directly hit by the housing crisis', National Housing Federation, 23 September 2019: https://www.housing.org.uk/news-and-blogs/news/1-in-7-people-in-england-directly-hit-by-the-housing-crisis

Mike Winters, 'Rent prices will keep going up in 2023 – here's what to expect', CNBC, 28 September 2022: https://www.cnbc.com/2022/09/28/how-much-higher-rent-will-go-in-2023-according-to-experts.html

p. 124
Kieran Yates, *All the Houses I've Ever Lived In: Finding Home in a System That Fails Us* (London: Simon & Schuster, 2023).

p. 127
Patrick Butler, 'Black, Asian and disabled tenants "more likely to face housing discrimination"', Guardian, 26 May 2021: https://www.theguardian.com/society/2021/may/26/black-asian-disabled-tenants-more-likely-face-housing-discrimination

p. 140
Housing affordability in England and Wales: 2022, Office for National Statistics, 22 March 2023: https://www.ons.gov.uk/peoplepopulationandcommunity/housing/bulletins/housingaffordabilityinenglandandwales/2022

Katherine Schaeffer, 'Key facts about housing affordability in the U.S.', Pew Research Center, 23 March 2022: https://www.pewresearch.org/short-reads/2022/03/23/key-facts-about-housing-affordability-in-the-u-s/

Stephen Johnson, 'How much you need to earn to be considered among the top half of Australian income earners – and the "middle" salary in YOUR industry', Daily Mail, 15 December 2021: https://www.dailymail.co.uk/news/article-10311107/Australian-average-salary-Bureau-Statistics-need-earn-average.html

Michael Yardney, 'The latest median property prices in Australia's major cities', Property Update, 2 November 2023: https://propertyupdate.com.au/the-latest-median-property-prices-in-australias-major-cities/

p. 146
Emily Henson, *Create: Inspiring Homes That Value Creativity Before Consumption* (London: Ryland, Peters & Small, 2022).

Emily Henson, *Life Unstyled: How to Embrace Imperfection and Create a Home You Love* (London: Ryland, Peters & Small, 2016).

p.164
Ingrid Fetell Lee, *Joyful: The Surprising Power of Ordinary Things to Create Extraordinary Happiness* (London: Rider, 2018).

p. 175
Nathan H. Lents, 'Why Do Humans Make Art?' *Psychology Today*, 5 September 2017: https://www.psychologytoday.com/us/blog/beastly-behavior/201709/why-do-humans-make-art

p. 180
Linda Grant, *The Thoughtful Dresser: The Art of Adornment, the Pleasure of Shopping, and Why Clothes Matter* (London: Virago, 2009).

Girl Guide quilt, Changi, Far East Civilian Internee, Imperial War Museum, catalogue number EPH 9206: https://www.iwm.org.uk/collections/item/object/30088773

p. 204
Alice Vincent, *Why Women Grow: Stories of Soil, Sisterhood and Survival* (London: Canongate, 2023), p.XX.

Further reading

Municipal Dreams by John Boughton (Verso; London, 2019)

Skint Estate by Cash Carraway (Ebury; London, 2019)

Undercurrent by Natasha Carthew (Coronet; London, 2023)

Status Anxiety by Alain De Botton (Haimish Hamilton; London, 2004)

Uprooting by Marchelle Farrell (Canongate; London, 2023)

Joyful by Ingrid Fettell Lee (Ebury; London, 2018)

The Making of Home by Judith Flanders (Atlantic Books; London, 2015)

A Modern Way to Live by Matt Gibberd (Penguin; London 2021)

Twelve Moons by Caro Giles (Harper North; Manchester, 2023)

The Little Book of Colour by Karen Haller (Penguin Life; London, 2019)

Create by Emily Henson (Ryland Peters & Small; London 2022)

Life Unstyled by Emily Henson (Ryland, Peters & Small; London, 2016)

Living Rooms by Sam Johnson-Schlee (Peninsula Press; London, 2022)

Why Women Grow by Alice Vincent (Canongate; London 2023)

Shelter: How Australians Live by Kara Rosenlund (Penguin; Australia 2015)

Tenants by Vicky Spratt (Profile; London, 2022)

The Language of Things by Deyan Sudjic (Penguin; London, 2008)

The Not-So-Big House by Sarah Susanka

Our Country in Crisis by Kwajo Tweneboa (Trapeze; London, 2024)

This Is Home by Nathalie Walton (Hardie Grant; Australia, 2018)

How Art Can Make You Happy by Bridget Watson Payne (Chronicle Books; San Francisco, 2018)

Edna Walling and her Gardens by Peter Watts (Florilegium; 1991)

A Gardener's Log by Edna Walling (Anne O'Donovan (reprint), Melbourne, 1985)

The Beauty of Everyday Things by Soetsu Yanagi (Penguin; London 2018)

All The Houses I've Ever Lived In by Kieran Yates (Simon & Schuster; London, 2023)

Contributors

With many thanks to all of the *Home Matters* contributors:

Chapter 1
Dr Emma Svanberg (dremmasvanberg.com)

Chapter 2
Rebecca Proctor (rebeccaproctor.co.uk)
Alyson Walsh (thatsnotmyage.com)

Chapter 3
Patrick and Neri Williams (berdoulat.co.uk)
Kate Sessions (sessionsandco.com)

Chapter 4
Huma Qureshi (humaqureshi.co.uk)
Karen Haller (karenhaller.com)
Alice Begg and Robbie Humphries (humphriesandbegg.co.uk)

Chapter 5
Furnishing Futures (furnishingfutures.org)
Caro Giles (substack.com / @carogileswrites)

Chapter 6
Emily Henson (emilyhensonstudio.com)
Alex Lewis (comptonmarbling.co.uk)

Chapter 7
Kemi Lawson (thecornrow.com)
Chloe Ashby (chloeashby.com)
Sonia Pang (galleryathome.co.uk)

Chapter 8
Marchelle Farrell (marchellefarrell.com)

Picture Credits

Introduction

p. 8 Patrick and Neri Williams' eighteenth century home in Bath. This gallery was built to echo the gallery in the shop at the front of the building. Triangle patchwork check cotton quilt by Toast.

p. 9 Fashion writer Alyson Walsh's South London art deco flat.

p. 11 Top left: Kemi Lawson's living room in Stanmore, London. Wooly canvas by Pomax. Top right: Rebecca Proctor's kitchen in North Cornwall. Bottom left: Sonia Pang's bedroom in Usk, Wales. Bottom right: Huma Qureshi's first floor hallway in Barnet, London.

p. 16 Bedroom of art director and author Emily Henson in Margate, Kent.

Chapter 1

p. 18 Penny's bedroom in her South London home. Artwork by Sue Kemp, bought by Penny's mother in Texas in 1987.

p. 19 Penny's childhood home Badgers Wood, Mooroolbark, Melbourne, 1988. The original living room of the house as designed by Edna Walling in the 1930s. The same artwork by Sue Kemp.

p. 22 Penny's childhood home Badgers Wood. Top left: the original cottage, 1981. Top right: Penny's mother, Chrissy, in front of Badgers Wood in 1983. Bottom: after it was extended, in the same style and building materials as the original, 1982.

p. 27 Penny's South London home. Top left: Penny's bedroom with artwork by Charlotte Keates. Top right: the kitchen pinboard. Bottom left: the dining table with kitchen chairs from Badgers Wood. Bottom right: Penny's bedroom mantel, with artwork by Chloë Cheese.

p. 30 Penny's childhood home, Badgers Wood, 1989.

p. 37 Penny's front hallway of her 1930s terrace house in South London.

Chapter 2

p. 40 Ceramic artist Rebecca Proctor's home, near Bude, Cornwall. Styled by Ben Kendrick.

p. 41 Fashion writer Alyson Walsh's South London flat.

p. 43-52 Rebecca Proctor's Cornish home, with carpentry by her partner Andrew. Styled by Ben Kendrick.

p. 57-63 Alyson Walsh's South London flat.

p. 57 Above left: photo of Joy Division by Kevin Cummins. Below and above right: prints by Paul Catherall.

p. 58 Above left: Vitra ball clock by George Nelson (1949-1960).

Chapter 3

p. 64 Designer and shop owners Patrick and Neri Williams' home in an 18th century shop, Bath.

p. 65 Designer Kate Session's sons' bedroom in Flaxton, Yorkshire. Wall hanging by Caitlin Hinshelwood for Sessions & Co. Artwork. Owl Flight by Mark Hearld. Bird tree cushions by Mark Hearld for Sessions & Co. Finlay fox rug by Sew Heart Felt. Lego Hogwarts™ .

p. 68 Berdoulat shop, with original shop fittings from 1890, which sits at the front of Patrick and Neri's home in Bath.

p. 73 Patrick and Neri's pantry, which runs alongside the kitchen, with original Victorian shop storage.

p. 75 Patrick and Neri's kitchen. The shop lies on the other side of the far door. The gallery visible above is pictured on page 8. Kitchen and dining table designed by Patrick for Berdoulat.

p. 78-80 Kate Session's home in Flaxton, Yorkshire. Original BTC Hector dome wall light.

Chapter 4

Chapter 5

Babayan. Page 121 bottom left: folding oak desk by Urbansize and Ikea ÖRFJÄLL chair.

p. 126 Caro Giles' bedroom in Northumberland. The smallest room in the house. Ikea Saxhyttan lamp.

p. 129 The space Caro carved out for herself to write, on the landing.

p. 130 The living room which Caro repainted and rearranged while reclaiming the space as her own.

Chapter 6

p. 136 Bridle Farm, the home of interior stylist Alex Lewis and his wife Anneke in Somerset.

p. 137 The home of art director and author Emily Henson in Margate, Kent.

p. 141-147 Emily Henson's partially renovated 1950s bungalow in Margate, Kent. The loft space above Emily's kitchen will become a reading nook.

p. 151 The farmhouse kitchen in Alex and Anneke's Somerset home. The kitchen was built with enough space for a wheelchair to move between the units. The kitchen island was installed so that Anneke (while she was still walking and using sticks) would never be far from a surface to lean on. The original stone floors provide a completely flat surface throughout the ground floor. Behind the curtain at the back of the room lies Anneke's annexe, created out of the old bakehouse. It has an accessible bathroom and bedroom.

p. 154 Top pictures: the kitchen has two sinks, one directly beside the Aga, so that Anneke could fill the kettle without moving it and drain pasta without having to carry a heavy item across the room. Below: the original doorways, designed to accommodate livestock, made it possible to make this Grade II listed house accessible without losing original features.

p. 159 The stone floors and wide doors that are throughout the ground floor that make it possible for Anneke to access all the downstairs rooms.

p. 196 Marchelle's garden.

p. 201 Rebecca Proctor's Cornish garden.

p. 205 A side gate in the stone wall of Badgers Wood, Mooroolbark, Melbourne, 1981.

p. 208 Top left: Badgers Wood as originally designed by Edna Walling, 1981. Top right: Penny's brothers Pip and Ashley on the front lawn in front Badgers Wood, 1983. Bottom: the back of Badgers Wood from the Pergola at the bottom of the back lawn, mid-1980s.

Conclusion

p. 210 Kemi Lawson's front hallway in Stanmore, Greater London. Left: Toile Des Caraïbes wallpaper by Yaël & Valérie

p. 211 Rebecca Proctor's kitchen diner in North Cornwall.

p. 213 Badgers Wood, Mooroolbark, the day the Wincers moved out, 1989.

p. 214 Penny's mother's iris painting at their farm, after they left Badgers Wood, 1990.

p. 219 Penny's living room in South London. Sessions & Co. Wall-hanging by artist Mark Hearld. (Marimekko Pieni Siirtolapuutarha cushion designed by Maija Louekari.)

p. 233 Penny's brother Pip in the garden at Badger's Wood, 1981.

p. 239 Penny's desk in the corner of her living room, South London.

Back cover photograph

Rebecca Proctor's Cornish home. Styled by Ben Kendrick.

About the author

Penny Wincer is a writer and writing coach. Her first book, *Tender: The Imperfect Art of Caring* was published in 2020. She has written for *The Telegraph*, *BBC Radio 4*, *Red Magazine*, the *iPaper* and co-hosts the podcast *Not Too Busy To Write*. Penny spent 6 years working as a fashion photographer's assistant between New York and London, before becoming an interiors and lifestyle photographer, shooting for magazines and brands such as *Country Living*, *Living Etc*, *House Beautiful*, *Guardian Weekend* and many more. She has spent 15 years telling the visual stories of home. Penny lives in South London with her two children.

Acknowledgements

Home Matters began life with an email from my wonderful agent, Julia Silk, which started along the lines of 'Not to distract you from what you're working on, but how would you feel about pitching a book on thinking deeply about interiors?' I baulked, closed the email, and within 15 minutes could not stop jotting down notes about all the things I felt were missing from the conversation about homes. It's only thanks to her support and enthusiasm that this book is now in your hands.

On this journey right from the beginning, my brilliant editor Sarah Thickett gave me the most incredible encouragement and patience. It's been a joy to work with someone with a similar vision for what might be possible if we throw the rules away when it comes to interiors books. Equally, Alicia House was a dream collaborator. Thank you both for trusting me, backing me up on so many creative decisions and being such a pleasure to work with. Big thanks too, to Lianne Nixon for her beautiful cover illustration and to the whole team at Quadrille.

Huge thanks to every single one of the interviewees who invited me into their homes: Kate, Patrick and Neri, Rebecca, Aly, Huma, Alice and Robbie, Caro, Emily, Kemi, Sonia and Marchelle. And thank you to the two beneficiaries of Furnishing Futures who very kindly allowed me to tell a very small part of their stories. It is no small thing to have a photographer come into your private space, especially when they are asking very nosy questions. It is a privilege to share your experiences, thoughts and homes with readers.

I also want to give a special thanks to Alex and Anneke. The conversation that appears in this book turned out to be my last ever with Anneke. Anneke embraced so much of the philosophy behind *Home Matters*. I will cherish her words and the love she had for her home and her family, as well as her tenacity to make the absolute best out of a very raw deal. You will be so missed.

Huge thank you to the experts who gave me their time and thoughts on topics they know far more about than I do – most particularly Karen Haller, Emma Svanburg, Marchelle Farrell, Emily Henson and Chloe Ashby. And to Emily Wheeler, founder of Furnishing Futures; I am in awe of the work you do and I hope we can spread the message of the necessity, value and dignity of beautiful and comfortable homes, far and wide.

Once again, my lovely family have been very chill about me writing about my life: thank you Dad, Pip and Ash for letting me do my thing and encouraging me along the way. Dad – thank you for my first homes. I couldn't have asked for a better start in life.
To my mum, who died more than two decades ago now but who is imprinted in this book. Thank you for making Badgers Wood so incredibly special, not just for us, but for our extended family and friends too. It's a home that lives on in so many people's memories. Special thanks to Emily, Lucy and Georgie, as well as the rest of the Barker, Rogers and McDermott families. It has been a joy to write a little about Bickleigh Vale and what it meant to us. I will always be grateful for the extended family I gained from those years. Thank you also to Melissa for allowing me to visit Badgers Wood. It makes me so happy to know that it is in the hands of someone who adores it as much as we did.

The vast majority of the photographs were shot on the day of the interviews. But special thanks to Ben Kendrick and Hearst for allowing me to reproduce images I shot for *Country Living* magazine, of Rebecca Proctor's home, with styling by Ben Kendrick.

Writing a book that required in-person interviews around the country was no small feat as a parent and unpaid carer. Huge thank you to the Society of Authors for support in the form of the K. Blundell Trust Award, which helped pay for care for my disabled son while I spent many hours on the road. The Society of Authors plays a huge role in making it financially possible for UK based writers to publish high quality work, as well as being a trade union which gives free legal advice to its members and lobbies for authors' rights – we are very lucky to have you.

As always, I am hugely grateful for my writers' group for all their emotional, practical and writerly support: Ilona, Sarah, Nicola, Caro and Hannah. Where would I be without you?! Massive thanks too, to everyone who has continually championed my work online and in person, from readers, listeners of *Not Too Busy To Write* and other writers. Thank you for all your support!

To my kids: thanks for putting up with such an overstretched working mother, who is often distracted by words, even when she's not at her desk. I hope the home I have created for you is a joyful and loving as the one I was raised in (even if the garden is a bit of a mess).

There is another person without whom this book could quite literally not exist. There is no way I could have completed it without the support of Ruairi, who stepped in and looked after my children countless times, and very often at 5am when I had a long drive ahead of me. Thank you my love, for embracing the madness and always supporting my work.

Managing Director Sarah Lavelle
Commissioning Editor Sarah Thickett
Copy Editor Holly Kyte
Proofreader Marie Clayton
Designer Alicia House
Illustrator Lianne Nixon
Head of Production Stephen Lang
Production Controller Gary Hayes

Published in 2024 by Quadrille Publishing Limited.

Quadrille
52–54 Southwark Street
London SE1 1UN
quadrille.com

The publisher has made every effort to credit all the artists and designers whose
work appears incidentally in the book and will be more than happy to correct or
add any omissions in future reprints.

Cataloguing in Publication Data: a catalogue record for this book is available
from the British Library.

ISBN 978 1 83783 091 6

Printed in China